D1293998

BIBLE AND LITERATURE SERIES

Editor
David M. Gunn

WOMEN RECOUNTED

Narrative Thinking
and the God of Israel

JAMES G. WILLIAMS

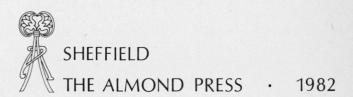

SHEFFIELD

THE ALMOND PRESS · 1982

BIBLE AND LITERATURE SERIES, 6

British Library Cataloguing in Publication Data:

Williams, James G.
  Women recounted: narrative thinking and the
  God of Israel. - (Bible and literature series,
  ISSN 0260-4493; 6)
  1. Women in the Bible
  I. Title   II. Series
  220.8'3054   BS680.W7

  ISBN 0-907459-18-8
  ISBN 0-907459-19-6 Pbk

Published by
The Almond Press
P.O. Box 208
Sheffield S10 5DW
England

Printed in Great Britain
by Redwood Burn Limited
Trowbridge, Wiltshire
1982

FOR KATHY

CONTENTS

9

ACKNOWLEDGMENTS

I would like first to acknowledge my debt to women and Scripture and women in Scripture, without whom this book could not have been written.

I am grateful to those who have helped and encouraged me, whether in this particular project or in other literary critical studies. James Ackerman has shown interest in my work and has been a facilitator of communication among many of us. Robert Polzin challenged my interpretive daring. Martin Buss urged me to hold on (like Jacob?) and continue what I was doing. Amanda Porterfield was a sensitive discussion partner as she and I conducted a fruitful graduate seminar, "The Feminine in Biblical and American Literarture." David Gunn, the general editor of Almond's Bible and Literature series, has shown confidence in me; his confidence and cooperative attitude have enhanced my research and writing. Others, such as Robert Alter, William Beardslee, Gerhard Neumann, and David Robertson, have affirmed my work at various stages along the way.

Of course, none are so dear to any person as those who are family or are related in friendship and religious community, for they offer the gift of continual trust and support without which inspiration cannot become realization. Not least of those dear to me is our oldest daughter, Katherine Yvonne, to whom this book is dedicated.

Syracuse, New York
July 9, 1982

Chapter I

ON BIBLICAL NARRATIVE:
PERSPECTIVE AND METHOD

WE ARE NOW in the process of taking a new look at sexual roles and institutions in western culture. Women are standing up to be counted, and many of us who feel this new cultural breeze are reviewing the accounts that are paradigmatic in our cultural and religious traditions. Not the least of these sources is the Bible, in which many stories of women are told, though some until recently have too seldom been recounted. They need to be recounted, but not simply as the mirrors of the history of a patriarchal, patrilinear society, for if Scripture is approached only as history, interpreters of Scripture are doomed to live in the past or, what amounts to the same thing, to try to reproduce the past in the present. This is impossible to do, and at any rate it denies the status of Scripture as inspired literature by divinizing a segment of the past and thus obstructing the divine voice in the present. Scripture is inspired only if it witnesses to the voice of the eternal Presence.

Of course, the stories of women cannot be recounted utterly apart from the history of the ancient Jews and the primitive church, for history is the necessary condition of what we know as human being. Yet what I propose here is a literary approach. Not that the Bible is only literature, any more than it is merely history. It is simply that in our time a certain kind of literary approach is committed to the integrity of the biblical text, refusing to see it reduced from a corpus to a hacked up corpse for the sake of reconstructing historical situations, sequences and events. Moreover, the literary approach offers the possibility of appreciating a dimension of the text that transcends the history in which it was composed. This dimension is centered in the function of a rich and various language, such as the multifaceted metaphor. As Lichtenberg said, "A metaphor is far more clever than its author" (F369). But I do not intend to argue that a literary approach is the same thing as accepting Scripture as divinely inspired. I hold rather that we are in a historical period when the literary perspective may be an entrée into questions of faith and theology such as the authority and inspiration of Scripture, while simultaneously granting a significant place to the questions, freedom, and creativity of both the reader and the biblical writer. Historical criticism has its own role in this perspective, as we shall see, but it should not dominate the way we look at the biblical text.

Let us return for a moment to the Bible as a source of western religion, morals, and culture. It is unfortunate, in my opinion, that the Bible has been so completely associated with religion and divinely given laws, whereas by contrast philosophy, the arts and political science are attributed to the Greeks and the Romans are given credit as mediators of greek culture. While such generalizations offer a partial truth, it is a neglected fact that Scripture coheres in various literary forms that are also vehicles of dynamic thinking about the world, humankind, society, and the divine source of all life. Most of it is, of course, committed thinking - thinking committed to faith in the creator and redeemer God of Israel or to the divine governance of the cosmos (as in much of the wisdom literature), and this thinking was bound to be affected by and use the literary conventions of the ancient near east. But ancient Israel also broke through to a new literary form, a kind of "fiction" which will be discussed in time.

One of Israel's great literary modes of thought and knowledge was the proverb and related forms. This "aphoristic" thinking was not original with her, but she developed it in strikingly creative ways (Williams, 1981). From time to time biblical scholars have examind the philosophical or cognitive side of biblical wisdom traditions (MacDonald; Beardslee[1]). Other areas of Hebrew thinking have also been examined (Frankfort, Boman, inter alios), but in the last two or three decades there has been relatively little stress on this aspect of biblical literature. A welcome exception is the recent book of Robert Alter, The Art of Biblical Narrative. He approaches biblical stories as a kind of "fiction" which conceives of meaning as a "process, requiring continual revision ...," as a mirror of " ... the uncertainties of life in history" (12, 27). He devotes an entire chapter to a discussion of "narration and knowledge," using the story of Joseph to illustrate the thesis "that fiction is a mode of knowledge ...." and that "fiction fundamentally serves the biblical writers as an instrument of fine insight into ... abiding perplexities of the human condition" (156, 176). Alter's pioneering literary critical work will be of great influence on this study as I treat biblical narrative as a mode of thinking and a way both of transmitting and arriving at knowledge.

The present study has two primary purposes. The literary critical purpose is to show that biblical narrative represents a dynamic mode of thinking and formation of knowledge. This thesis concerning narrative thinking will be textually grounded and instantiated by an investigation of stories about key feminine personages in the Hebrew Scriptures, the Old Testament Apocrypha, the New Testament and the New Testament Apocrypha. These are females who are symbolically significant in the accounts of Israel's - and the church's - destiny, origins, or chances for survival in the world. I hope this study will give birth to new insights into narrative thinking and how women count.

The second purpose is theological, and it will be fully articulated in the last chapter. It is to indicate and clarify the interrelationship of these biblical images of the feminine, the nature of language, and the meaning of the "God of Israel."

A. Narrative Thinking

To reiterate the literary thesis: biblical narrative represents a dynamic mode of thinking whose aesthetic properties support and enhance the process of arriving at knowledge. To think is to bring the intellectual faculties into play in order to arrive at ideas, judgments, conclusions concerning data, insights, etc. Thinking is not just a matter of searching for or focusing on abstractions. Indeed, this essay will be more concerned with a practical, experiential thinking, although abstract concepts are by no means to be precluded. The point is that in certain of its forms thinking is very close to feelings and commitments. Take, for example, the verbal expression "think of." This often means to remember, which may point to someone or something of great value to us.

I always think of my mother at this time of year.
We're thinking of you and past vacations that we've shared.

It sometimes signifies to discover or invent, both of which are associated with searching and often result in satisfaction or even elation.

I just thought of something!
I just thought of a way to do it!
He thought of a research plan that would enable him successfully to complete the experiment.

It may mean <u>considering the welfare</u> of someone or something (= caring, to be considerate).

She is so thoughtful of others. She always thinks of the other person.
He always thinks of his plants when it freezes.

Here "think of" is practically synonymous with sympathy and the expression of love. So thinking, though in some sense always an activity of the "mind," is not essentially divorced from feeling and volition. Indeed, it may be a way of mediating between rational purpose and emotional concerns, as in <u>narrative</u>.

I understand narrative in the generic sense as a mode of expression that works more or less as Aristotle defined poetry or tragedy in the Poetics (Aristotle: esp. VII-XI). It is characteristically communicated through a plot that links the beginning, middle, and end of a series of events. The "middle" includes conflict and the movement to resolve conflict. Resolution or proximate resolution is typically preceded by "recognition," what Aristotle called "anagnörisis," a "change from ignorance to knowledge, producing love or hate between the persons destined by the poet for good or bad fortune" (XI). The narration of a story creates a fictional world, whether large or limited, depending on the type and scope of tale to be told. Aristotle called this world-creation "mimesis," often translated "imitation." However, "representation" would be a better rendering, for the philosopher did not mean the exact reproduction of actual persons and events (II). It is simply that a credible world must be established as a frame of reference for the audience or reader. Of course, all fictional works require some degree of "suspension of disbelief" on the part of the audience, especially those that are perceived as fantasy, fairy tale, and the like. But as Wayne Booth has point out, "the work itself ... must fill with its rhetoric the gap made by the suspension of my own beliefs" (Booth: 112). Furthermore, if the distance is too great between the readers' beliefs, on the one hand, and the values or beliefs they are manipulated into accepting, on the other, they may have the experience of becoming "mock readers" who cannot respect themselves (Booth: 139). Thus there must normally be a representation of basic aspects of the audience's world, the most important part of which is beliefs or value-based expectations. A story-teller, in varying degrees, both makes and represents a world.

The storytelling activity inevitably entails the use of a temporal continuum, in two senses. First, the story takes time to tell. How much time depends on the type of story. One will not usually attempt to approximate the time span in the story to the time taken for the telling. Events and periods may be summarily collapsed in the narration, or if important enough for the plot they may be stretched out beyond their probable duration in actuality. Second, the tale told must proceed from beginning to end through sequences of changes which center in problems and problems met, if not always solved. Modern and contemporary exceptions to this general rule are simply that, exceptions which deliberately cast aside temporal coherence. They are examples of "anti-narrative," or as has been said of Kafka's work, of "anti-metaphor" whose denial of representation seeks to make the literary work itself its own metaphor (Allemann).

The story of Jacob, Genesis 25.19-35.29, provides a good illustration of these features of narrative as thinking. The broad perimeters of the story encompass the blessing of Jacob, his journey from the promised land and his return as one who has realized his destiny. There are conflicts, revelations of special destiny, helpers and adversaries at crucial points, winning of a boon (blessing and a new name), and re-entry into the homeland. The Jacob story is a kind of ancient israelite comedy. Besides being often ironically funny, the plot moves Jacob from a slave of Laban on foreign soil to an apex where he escapes and is reconciled with his "world," that is, with his brother and his God. After his struggle with the mysterious adversary who blesses him and gives him a new name, he names the site of the struggle Peniel, "face of God" (32.31). When he is reunited and reconciled with Esau, he says that seeing his brother is "like seeing the face of God" (33.10).

In the Jacob story we see, then, the dramatically significant beginning, middle, and end of a series of events, which proceeds through a temporal continuum and centers in conflict and resolution of conflict. Considered as a kind of narrative "geography" the middle point is the boundary of the land of Canaan, the holy space that Jacob leaves and must re-enter (see Fishbane). The context of the departure and re-entry is fear of his brother Esau as he flees and anxiety that Esau will take revenge as he returns to Canaan. In both departure and return Jacob has a decisive numinous experience before he crosses a border. The first experience occurs in Gen 28, conveying the dream revelation that reaffirms the divine promises to the ancestors, and the second in Gen 32 brings him a renewed blessing and a new name, Israel. A diagram of the plot movement:

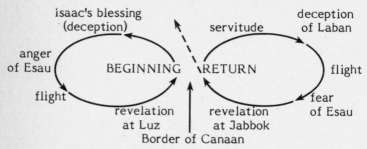

But after the return to the land, the plot opens up again with new conflicts (rape of Dinah, Joseph and his brothers).

Concerning the story's world of values, it undoubtedly conveys many beliefs and customs from premonarchic and monarchic times that an audience in the monarchic period could accept: the God of the fathers who guides his chosen clans, patriarchal authority, marriage customs, etc. But an ancient israelite audience would most certainly have had to suspend disbelief in some aspects of the story. Three of the characters engage in forms of deception: Jacob, Rebecca, and Laban. Especially damaging, if this be viewed as a didactic narrative recommending moral models and values, is Jacob's penchant for trickery. We see him engaging in unscrupulous opportunism, though Esau is rather a loutish slave to his immediate needs (25.29-34). Jacob presents himself in disguise as his brother, instigated by his mother (27.1-29), and he uses homeopathic magic to build up his flock at Laban's expense (31.25-43; not that Laban didn't deserve it). It has been held that Jacob is no longer a trickster after having been transformed from "Jacob" to "Israel" at the Jabbok. But to the contrary, after the reconciliation with Esau he lies to him about rejoining him in Seir (33.14, 18). We have evidence from the biblical traditions that some who heard the Jacob story with a concentrated moral seriousness rather than the dramatic sense of a good story were not sanguine about Jacob the rogue. In the form of a divine lawsuit speech, Hosea proclaims that Yahweh will punish Jacob "according to his ways" (Hos 12.3). the prophet then proceeds to refer to parts of the Jacob account that we know from Genesis. This includes an evidently unfavorable comparison of Jacob to Moses which plays on the verb "sāmar," "keep, guard, watch" (12.13-14).

... and Israel served for a wife,
and for a wife he kept (sheep) [ûbeʔiššâ šāmār].
And by a prophet Yahweh brought Israel up from Egypt,
and by a prophet he was kept [ûbenābîʔ nišmār].

Jacob guarded sheep for the sake of having a wife, but Moses guarded Israel!

Jeremiah exploits Jacob's name in decrying an incorrigible people (9.3):

Let each one beware of his neighbor!
Distrust every brother!
For every brother is indeed deceitful [cāqôb yacaqōb],
every neighbor deals in slander.

John Bright translates the third stich, "For every brother's crafty as Jacob," and says that cāqôb yacaqōb is an unmistakable pun on Jacob's name (Bright: 67, 71-72).

But that the Jacob story is a key narrative portion of the Torah attests that it was appreciated by many in ancient Israel. Why would any israelite audience have suspended ordinary moral conventions in transmitting and doubtlessly enjoying these tales of a rascal's deeds? Or why not have done a bit of censoring in order to put this eponymous ancestor in a better light? I would offer two reasons for this tolerance of moral ambiguity. One is that ancient Israelites, like audiences in most times and places, could, if forewarned by certain conventions, suspend their ordinary scruples and find such a story both entertaining and therapeutic, especially if it is a comedy. The therapy resides in letting the ambiguities of existence have free play, in seeing deceivers deceived (including Jacob), the favored one flee and struggle, the blessed one both generous and sly. "If there's hope for Jacob, there's hope for me." Perhaps one may not say that, but many may _feel_ that way. The second reason is bound up with Israel's peculiar situation in the world as represented in her literature. As we shall see in the stories about women, the tenuousness of Israel's situation in the world leads sometimes to subterfuge and various kinds of deception for the sake of the chosen one and the new divinely given order in the world. This deception is often committed by an important female, and the imagery of the feminine is bound up with the way Israel viewed its origins and prospects as well as the very nature of language.

Finally, what about the Jacob story as a mode of thinking and vehicle of knowledge? It is, in fact, a perfect exemplification of Alter's concept of hebrew narrative as meaning in process. It is a form of remembering, "thinking of," which gives rise to reflection, "thinking on." It directs the hearer to the boundary, to the line separating the land of promise from the "outside," from exile. It leads the imagination towards ends that are both ahead and behind: the fulfillment of the blessing is yet to be realized, and for it to be realized one is led back to where one was before (the homeland which is not yet one's own). It evokes a journey with Jacob/Israel whose concrete language and movements are a voyage of insights:

- That being divinely blessed is a reality, but nonetheless ambiguously so, in history. It is not a state attained without daring interpretation, as seen in Rebecca's understanding of the oracle (25.23; 27) and Jacob's inference as to what had happened at the Jabbok (32.31; cf. v. 25, "a man" [heb: ʔîš] and v. 29, "with God and with men").

- That God's blessings are not easily won, yet they are given, and that a long journey is required to receive them.

- That Israel, as represented by Jacob, wins his way in the world only by persistence, by "holding on" (25.19-26; 32.23-33), but he can hold on to his blessing only if he shares it with his brother (33.11; see Williams, 1978: 255).

- That "seeing God" and making peace with one's brother (= other self? other side?) are somehow related (32.31; 33.10).

- That the story of Jacob/Israel does not end with his safe return to the land, for the story moves on to conflict with the Shechemites (Gen 34) and renewed threat to the promises (the Joseph story). And when the Joseph story ends, it too is reopened: "Now there arose a new king over Egypt who knew nothing of Joseph" (Ex 1.8). And so the story continues.

- That whatever the dangers in the journey of Jacob/Israel the essential thing to think of and upon is Yahweh's promise, "Behold, I am with you and I will keep you wherever you go ...." (Gen 28.15).

In summary, narrative thinking is a mode of consciousness which brings the intellectual faculties into play in order to arrive at conclusions, insights, and whatever may be significant as fact. It is a way of valuing and remembering by laying out sequences and themes in a coherent temporal continuum. As narrative thinking this mode of apprehending existence proceeds dramatically and imaginatively through a continuity of events (which characteristically include incongruities and discontinuities in biblical narrative) towards a resolution of whatever problems arise to challenge or obstruct the original premises of the plot. It therefore must establish a credible world in which the reader can feel "at home." Roughly to compare narrative thinking to abstract philosophical thinking, it is as house to structure or as body to anatomy.

Excursus:
Narrative and Aphoristic Thinking Compared

Parable and aphorism have come to the forefront of theological discussion in the last ten to fifteen years (Beardslee: ch. 3; Miller: ch. 6; Crossan, 1973 and 1976; Williams 1981; and others). It may therefore be appropriate to say a word about narrative thinking as compared to aphoristic thinking. Aphoristic forms - gnomes, sentences, maxims, reflections (e.g., Pascal's pensées), etc. - are of interest in the modern era chiefly because they offer the possibility either of moral education or the expression of a new vision of things without advocacy of a system or being caught up in the grand coherence of narrative, be it history or fiction (see Beardslee, 30; Williams, 1981: ch. 4). To put my point succinctly, aphoristic discourse neither constructs a world nor takes time. Obviously it "takes time" in the literal sense - both in that it requires time to express and that it is applied in circumstances which are perforce temporal. But the aphoristic form typically seeks by its characteristic brevity to reduce the sense of time taken, and it expresses the timeless universal, the general truth, unless it employs paradox to undercut prevailing beliefs. Aphorism moves the mind to look into a small aspect of an accepted order or to deconstruct the received state of things on the basis of a vision that requires a counter-order.

Aphorism is a genre of conflict (Neumann, 1976a: Einleitung; 1976b). It is, however, not like the conflict inherent in narrative. It does not describe conflict or represent it within the form; it represents the conflict itself by its very form, the conflict of order and anti-order, thought and feeling, representation and paradox, topia and utopia. One of the polarities may be concealed or only intimated, but the tension may be so much the more effective as a result. If nothing else, there looms before the aphoristic form a situation, a case that has to be filled in if it is to have a concrete meaning. For example, the folk saying, "a bird in the hand is worth two in the bush," takes on meaning when one contemplates a situation of risking something already possessed for the sake of something putatively better.

The most common form of aphoristic thinking is the generalization that either conceals or only hints at the particular situation out of which it is formed.

> Treasures of wickedness do not profit,
> but righteousness delivers from death. [Prov 10.2]

> Who digs a pit will fall in it,
> Who rolls a stone, it will roll back on him. [Prov 26.27]

> In general we seek the unconditioned [Unbedingte]
> and find only conditions [Dinge]. [Novalis][2]

Prov 26.27 is a proverb about moral retribution, perhaps intimating the often enigmatic nature of retribution. Novalis's sentence from the "mixed remarks" (Vermischte Bemerkungen) goes even further than the proverb in speaking of life's paradoxical character. However, language itself is not here an instance of paradox; rather it speaks about paradox.

The topic of paradox brings us to the type of aphoristic speech which does not offer a glimpse into an order of things, but counters the accepted assumptions with a vision or intuition about another reality, or another dimension of reality. Here paradox becomes part of the language itself. Many of the parabolic sayings of Jesus represent the disorienting effect of the arriving rule of God.

> To him who has will more be given; and from him who
> has not even what he has will be taken away. [Mk 4.25]

A master of radical paradox was Kafka, whose "sliding paradoxes" sometimes seem to represent themselves as the "what," the content of Kafka's vision. One of Kafka's aphorisms is related in an interesting fashion to Novalis's fragment, and it shows how paradox becomes part of the language used [Betrachtungen, #16]:

Who seeks does not find, but who doesn't seek is found.

Neumann has made the interesting comment that "seeking and finding as point of departure and conclusion of a 'way' outlines a field of imagery that shapes the context of the process of knowing from the biblical tradition [Matt 7.8/Lk 11.10] to Franz Kafka" (Neumann, 1976b: 290). Kafka takes the ancient aphoristic truth and "glides" into a paradox that is not simply a reversal of ordinary logic or opinion ("who doesn't seek finds"), but a whole new orientation. The greatest "activity" becomes "passivity." Is this something positive (God/the truth/your true self will come to you)? Or is it negative (you are sure to be found out, you can't escape from - whatever)?

There is a third kind of aphorism which is found only in the modern period, as far as I know. It conceals or hints at the general by expressing the particular. It exposes an I, a personal voice and particularities of existence, but the impression given is that a general truth is there, perhaps in the hearer's mind waiting to be evoked. Like this "thought" of Stanislaw Lec:

Why do I write these short jests?
Because I lack the words. [Lec: 52]

And to return to Kafka, there is his much discussed sentence,

A cage went in search of a bird. [Betrachtungen, #16].

Something is suggested here that implies an insight into Kafka's soul and perhaps the human condition generally. But what is it? Is the bird a cipher for Kafka's "I," as some have thought? (Neumann, 1973: 465) But the "I" could just as easily be the cage which seeks to imprison its own better self (soul? freedom?). Kafka, in giving himself to the "thing," to the particular, to the intensively and paradoxically personal, was perhaps trapped in his own ego. Yet he was not far from the insight of the mystic Meister Eckhart,

Only the hand that erases can write the true thing.[3]

So aphoristic discourse has no temporal continuum; it intends to speak of the timeless or to tear asunder a coherent sense of time. It does not link a beginning, middle and end of plotted action, but offers a glimpse of order or of counter-order. It presupposes belief, which it either supports with metaphors or principles or opposes in paradox (gk. "paradoxon," "beyond" or "contrary to opinion"). It is especially apposite to those elements of experience that are felt to be unsuitable for the narrative coherence of story or the abstract coherence of a conceptual system.

Be it timeless truth, the workings of a transcendent reality that is beyond story and system, or the quest for a new language for a new age (Neumann, 1976b), aphoristic speaking and thinking function differently from narrative and reflect a different sort of consciousness. It may be that aphoristic discourse becomes more attractive in intellectually uncertain times (so Grenzmann in Neumann, 1976a: 207). We know that in in the period when the israelite salvation history was basically unopen to revision, there emerged many great aphoristic forms and aphorists (Proverbs, Kohelet, Sirach, Jesus, Abot). In the final chapter I shall raise the question whether the religious and intellectual uncertainties of our own epoch make aphorism more appropriate for marking out a religious way.

In any event, this book by way of contrast will focus on narrative thinking, with special reference to the feminine figures who have an important role in Israel's sense of itself as the bearer of a divine order linking the beginning and end of time in a revelatory continuity.

B. Fiction, History and Myth

1. Fiction and History

Every human expression is "fictive" in some sense, which is to say that we shape and refract the "facts," the givens of our worlds as we think them and utter them. The basic form of history must be narrative, otherwise it has no coherence. In this sense the historian tells a story, which by definition must be shaped by the teller. He or she decides on it form and sub-forms (how to handle speeches, intentions of human subjects, matters of philosophy or ideas that do not lend themselves readily to narration, etc.). Thus even modern critical historiography is "fiction" to the extent that data do not interpret themselves and the historian relates a kind of story.[4] Or to put it another way, every history as told or written must be made. The common latin etymology of fact, fiction, fictive, and fictile is suggestive. But there are differences among the things made. It matters if one focuses on actual experiences that have occurred (history) as contrasted with the refashioning of experiences in a manner that does not require belief in corresponding events outside the story (fiction). When Nathaniel Hawthorne constructed a puritan world populated with authentic puritan characters, that exact world and its characters never existed, nor will it ever come to be as far as we know. Not that a story like "The Scarlet Letter" is not built up out of the "matter" of an actual puritan world, with its calvinist theology, social strictures, uncertain guilt-ridden consciences, etc. Hawthorne paints portraits based on or suggested by actual people and characteristics as assimilated through the vision that moves him to write. He catches the essence of such a society and certain of its individuals according to the logic of his own concerns and way of seeing things. But whatever of history and historical persons that went into the depiction of Hester Prynne, for example, there never was such a heroine whose emblem, the letter A for "adultery," came to be understood as standing for "angel"; who believed:

> that at some brighter period, when the world had grown ripe for it, in Heaven's own time, a new truth would be revealed, in order to establish the whole relation between man and woman on a surer ground of happiness.
>
> [Hawthorne: 225]

This relation of history and fiction has been discussed at length by Ricoeur. He sketches their intersection, but he notes that history reveals what may occur on the basis of what has occurred, whereas fiction, in dealing with the "unreal," discloses what it means to be a human being in history. History is the mode of the "possible," fiction is the mode of the "essential," that is, of what is essential in human historicity. "Historicity" is the main link between history and fiction. This will be taken up shortly.

2. Literary Criticism and Historical Studies

To "mean" something is to point to or to signify - to give a sign that can in principle be received as communicating something. This basic meaning of "meaning" is apparent in the french "signifier," "signification," as well as in the german "bedeuten," "Bedeutung," which are formed from the root "deuten," to point to, signify. But much more than this must be said about meaning. Meaning requires someone giving a sign of something to someone else (an actual or imagined audience) in a situation. The someone else and the situation and what they and the sign-giver share in the way of signs form the context. The context offers the possibilities and

25

restraints of what may be signified and how it may be done.

This is to say, in short, that the necessary condition of meaning is context. There are different sorts of contexts, but here we shall focus on historical context, which has become a debated issue in contemporary biblical scholarship. A "paradigm shift" has occurred for many biblical scholars, leading them to engage in literary interpretation rather than historical criticism (Robertson, 1977: 4). Many other exegetes have opposed this shift to the point of scorning it, so it is evident that major emotional and professional investments reside in the commitment to historically oriented criticism or to literary criticism.

"New Criticism," structuralism, and deconstructionism have shared a primary concern with linguistic and underlying generative structure, with little or no consideration of historical context. Chomsky, for example, ignores extralinguistic context in his linguistic (or "grammatical") analysis (see Polzin, 1980: 4; 213 n.1). Robertson views the task of the literary critic as a voyage within the literary work itself and its kindred works. Speaking of literary conventions he says:

> We can say that a work of literature is a hypothetical world, the clues for the understanding of which come from within the work itself. These clues, however, can be understood only by reference to the genre to which the work belongs. Therefore we arrive at the conclusion that the decisive clues for interpreting any piece of literature come from other works of literature. [1977: 9]

For Robertson this means that the only important contexts are literary, so one must move out from a single work to related works in world literature. But how could one possibly know which works were related unless knowledge or theory of historical contexts were established? Robertson's own comparison of Exodus 1-15 and Euripides' play, "The Bacchae," (with a brief excursus on the gospel of Mark) is a case in point (Robertson, 1977: ch. 2). Even though he attempts a purely literary analysis and comparison of these works, it is clear throughout that his own historical knowledge is a constraint that both binds him and gives him some of his clues. When he says that "no convincing evidence exists to suggest that biblical authors or editors considered" Ex 1-15 isolable from the ensuing narrative (17) he betrays the knowledge that "The Bacchae" has one author, whereas Exodus may have more than one author and redactor. The

intimation that a literary work may not only reflect a tradition (as greek tragedy surely does), but shows the tradition
at work in multiple voices, changes the "meaning" of the
work necessarily. Once you know this, you are constrained to
render account of it.

At another point Robertson reflects (1977: 28):

> When we remember that Dionysian worship involved the
> sacrifice of an animal considered by the community to
> be a substitute for Dionysus himself, another and greater
> irony appears: Pentheus dies as a scapegoat and,
> therefore, as a surrogate for the very god he rejects.

He gives here the kind of information about Dionysus worship
that makes up the stuff of sociological and historical study. It
is necessary to the knowledge that sees the irony, that is, the
meaning of the work.

I would argue that the necessary condition of establishing
literary meaning must be historical in two senses. First, ac-
knowledgment of the historicity of human existence. Everyone belongs to "history" in the sense of having a heritage and
certain possibilities, whether they be few or many. All of us
are subject to finitude and find it frustrating, so that there
are scarcely any humans who do not have stories or histories
of how certain personae - gods or men - have faced their
fate. Everyone exists in time, and so seeks to remember the
past, which brings happiness or regret; or tries to anticipate
the future, which is an object of hope or anxiety. All humans
are, in short, caring creatures, and care is a function of
symbol-making animals who deal with situations. Robertson's
comment on the dionysian sacrificial rites in relation to
Pentheus' death in "The Bacchae" is the notation of a
historical fact for the sake of getting at the historicity of
Euripides' play. The playwright cares about something -
Robertson holds that this is an indictment of Dionysus
intended to evoke the "adult emotions" of "ambivalence
toward self, others, and the gods" and to instill the "adult
lessons" that not only my enemy and I but also the gods are
both good and bad. (1977: 30) To take another instance, when
the speaker in Emily Dickinson's poem identifies herself as
the lover and bride of God -

Title divine - is mine!
The wife - without the sign! [#1072]

* * * *

27

He touched me, so I live to know
That such a day - permitted so,
I groped upon his breast -
It was a boundless place to me .... [#506]

- it mades a considerable difference to know something of Dickinson's life and modes of self-presentation, and of the restricted literary possibilities for women in the 19th century (see A. Douglas: esp. chs. 1-3). She had no outlet for her unconventional religious tendencies and no sisterly precursor to serve as a paradigm of the kind of woman writer that it was her gift to be. Whatever the factors that led to her becoming a recluse, it is clear that she viewed herself as a kind of vocational virgin of God and the servant of some new Self that was aborning. (See Porterfield: ch. 7) She - or she as her human and divine personae - had to be her own audience.

The other necessary historical aspect of literary meaning is knowledge or helpful theory as to how the tradition works that transmits the literary work. How, why and when are works composed, and out of what problematics? How did the audiences and transmitter view the works?[5] If it is not possible to arrive at knowledge, as is so frequently the case, then hypothesis is useful as long as it is recognized for what is is. Suppose, for instance, that one held the hypothesis that the book of Ruth was composed during the period of developing exclusivism and rejection of intermarriage during the post-exilic reforms of Nehemiah and Ezra (c. 450-400 BC). This dating of the book would certainly not exhaust what it signifies - far from it, as we shall see. But it could be helpful to establish this as a possible historical context. It seems, in fact, that in the exilic and postexilic periods there emerged a new interest in the ancestral era as part of the re-interpretation of Israel's identity vis-à-vis the nations (see Sanders: 102-3). The anonymous "Isaiah" of Babylon, prophesying about 550-540 BC, was evidently the first of the great biblical prophets to refer to Abraham and Sarah (Isa 41.8; 51.2). (This is, of course, according to our received biblical text.) The book of Job, which is exilic or postexilic, is situated in a patriarchal, non-israelite social setting (Job is an Edomite). In the happy ending of Job his three daughters are given names signifying material and spiritual blessing (Dove, Cinnamon, Horn of Eye-Shadow), whereas the restored sons remain anonymous. Moreover, the daughters are allotted an inheritance with their brothers, which is unique in the Hebrew Scriptures but for which there are parallels in ancient Canaan and the world of Homer (Fohrer: 544-45; Pope: 292-93). Likewise there appears to be in Ruth a deliberate archaizing, an imaginative return to the time of origins. To know of this archaizing, at least as a possibility, necessarily affects interpretation of Ruth, especially if the period of composition was as already indicated. But in order to "know" one must have historical knowledge or useful historical hypothesis. Without it, one misses a good part of the author's creativity and the historicity that engages us in our own caring.

If historical knowledge is a necessary condition of literary meaning, the _sufficient_ condition is the step of entering into the language world of the text itself.[6] One needs first of all to determine the _genre_ of the writing to be interpreted. Historical knowledge will contribute to understanding of genre, but the essential thing at this point of the discussion is that one cannot find apple seeds by cutting up oranges. So also one does not find novels in fairy tales, scientific method in myths of creation, or historical facts in conventional forms concerned with repeating archetypes. Let me illustrate by reference to the "wife-sister" stories (Gen 12.10-20; 20; 26.1-11). At one time some cuneiform scholars thought that the wife as sister of the patriarch reflected law and social practices in the mesopotamian world of the ancestors. Recently this inference has been disproved, and the only reasonable conclusion, in my estimation, is that the wife-sister scene is a literary convention which the biblical storyteller employs to suggest significant themes in the account of Israel's origins. (See Williams, 1980a: 108-9, 111, 116-19.) In other words, the wife-sister scenes do not provide historical or sociological data in the ordinary sense because the narrative genre is a literary language which expresses the allegorical and symbolic aspects of the author's historicity and religious concerns.

Of course, entering into the language world of the text is an historical act in the sense that our historicity impels us to the interpretive act. But in the text itself there are meanings that are not exhausted by the historical genesis of the text. This is a basic principle for the theoretical foundation of this book: historical situations may be the occasions of meaning, but they do not exhaust what a given image, symbol or work means. This study holds that the religious meaning of images of the feminine cannot be reduced to the fact that ancient Israel was a patriarchal society and that women had little social, political, and (undoubtedly) literary authority. Images, symbols, and texts, like Lichtenberg's metaphor, are often more clever than their authors or historical occasions. The historical boundaries of the genesis of the Bible cannot be the final word in our interpretive conclusions.

Peter Berger has made a sociological point relevant to this discussion of the history-transcending potential of metaphorical language. He says that "bad faith is that form of false consciousness in which the dialectic between the socialized self and the self in its totality is lost to consciousness" (Berger: 93). My argument is that the metaphorical power of certain texts represents something akin to "the self in its totality." Whatever the social status of women in ancient Israel, they are important in some stories in which they are expressions of that "other self," or self in its totality that our religious and literary traditions have forgotten - not "thought of."

Since this is a literary study of scripture, it is not primarily concerned with history as the necessary condition of interpretation. I shall, however, touch here and there on the connection between historical context and literary imagination, and in ch. V (C.1.) I shall deal with the "imaginative structure" of thought and expression which was sharpened and informed by the experience of exile.

3. Myth and Biblical Prose

There has been considerable dispute over the word "myth" as applied to biblical stories and figures (Rogerson: 174-89). It has become a widely employed term in religious studies for a number of reasons. As theologians and comparative religionists have broken away from christian parochialism and the necessity of judeo-christian presuppositions, "myth" has been a handy word for describing a basic pattern of religious expression: the web of affective and effective symbols and stories of a religious tradition. "Religion" is too broad, and at any rate it often carries the connotation of ritual or devotional practices. "Story" does not have strong enough affective connotations and symbolic associations.

However, the word carries with it a mortgage of many historical and linguistic problems. First, and probably least serious in the academy, myth has become synonymous with falsehood in popular usage. This stems fron ancient jewish reactions to paganism and specifically from the negative use of the term in the New Testament to refer to false stories of

30

gods, to pagan (gnostic?) genealogies and doctrines (I Tim 1.4; 4.7; II Tim 4.4; Tit 1.14; II Peter 1.16).

Next we get into the question of genre. Since "myth" is derived from the greek "mythos," "tale," and came to be employed with reference to stories of the gods, is it appropriately used for interpreting a literature that has very few stories of the gods? The "myths" or stories of the gods throughout the mediterranean-middle eastern world were predicated on an understanding of reality whose model was natural phenomena and the seasonal cycles. By contrast, the biblical writers characteristically intimate, or affirm, a God who is transcendent, who is "other" than the cosmos, and who has no story except his relation to Israel. The model of existence in the larger context of the biblical tales is that of a covenant. As a model of existence it has three primary features: (a) Recounting the past and present relationship of the covenant partners. (b) Exchanging promises and vows, which orient the parties to the future. The covenant ethos, or divinely based moral strictures, is rooted in this exchange. (c) God guiding and protecting Israel in return for Israel's obedience and faithfulness.

Israel's covenant tradition gave rise to the world's first historiography, the project of narrating the coherent, continuous, continually revised story of a people. The inner workings of this historiography were born of the combination of covenant story, future-orientation, and affirmation of the divine providence.

The kind of narrative that emerged with ancient israelite religion and culture is far removed from myth as "stories of the gods" (see introduction to chs. II and IV). Biblical narrative exhibits a supple, often subtle openness and attunement to ambiguity which one does not find in myth. The latter undergirds an enclosed world in which earthly events and figures correspond, or are fated to correspond, to realities and decrees in the heavenly world. On the other hand, we see in Scripture the weighty place of human interpretation in the struggle for the God-given destiny, as in Jacob's attribution of significance to his experience at the Jabbok; or Joseph's interpretation of the meaning of the betrayal by his brothers and his sojourn in Egypt (Gen 45.4-8), an interpretation of which the narrator clearly approves but which is never directly confirmed in reported words of God. Sometimes things happen "by accident" (Gen 26.8), but they turn out according to God's will.

31

I shall therefore avoid using the word myth as a description of any kind of biblical narrative. There is one difficulty with this self-imposed restriction. We shall consider certain functions of the biblical heroines which are basic to religious experience and symbolic expression. These are the representations of origins, destiny, and the movement from one to the other. I had intended to utilize the adjective "mythical" to denote these functions, but "symbolic" will be used instead. "Symbolic" means that the biblical women to be studied are both concrete in their dramatic vividness and abstract in the ideas they encompass as they mediate the reality of Israel to the reader of the text.

In this study I follow the lead of Robert Alter in viewing biblical narrative as prose fiction. This is not to deny that elements of myth, epic, legend, folk tale, etc. are present in biblical prose. It is simply that the new and dynamic elements of biblical narrative, as compared to ancient near eastern narrative forms, render ordinary literary categories unsuitable. Frank Kermode had made a point similar to Alter's in distinguishing myth from fiction. He says that fictions serve a process of discovery, they are "agents of change," whereas myths establish stability and undergird absolutes (Kermode: 39; cf. Dunne: 7). Of course, in his "The Sense of An Ending" Kermode is referring to modern fiction, and in context his specific examples are drawn from Shakespeare's "King Lear." Moreover, his criterion that fictions can degenerate into myth "whenever they are not consciously held to be fictive" (ibid.) cannot be applied without qualification to biblical narrative. Yet insofar as biblical narrative spins out a story in process, continually being opened up and revised as it gives expression to the new people of God, the vicissitudes of history, and the God who is never held within a name or story, Alter's approach comes very close to Kermode's concept of fiction. Is this fiction comparable to the modern novel? In some respects, yes. Some of the ancient israelite story-tellers and a few of the early christian writers had a sense of dramatic contingency, existential uncertainties, irony of language and action, and subtleties of character that anticipate some of the important features of modern western fiction. But in other respects, the answer is no. Biblical fiction is attuned to the historical existence and concerns of the people Israel; it thus reveals the historicity of its authors and tradents, who collected great blocks of material to form a larger story of Israel. So if this fiction is not myth, epic, or legend, yet cannot be understood as analogous to modern prose fiction except with considerable caution, how should it be comprehended?

Herbert Schneidau provides an orienting insight when he calls Genesis and parts of the story of David "the birth of a new kind of historicized fiction which moves steadily away from the motives and habits of the world of legend and myth" (Schneidau: 215). Indeed, "historicized fiction" is a phrase applicable to other narrative segments of Scripture. But as Alter says, it is helpful to refine Schneidau's insight and think in terms of both "historicized fiction" and "fictionalized history" (Alter: 25, 32-33). This refinement retains the notion of making, of shaping that has gone into the creative achievement of the ancient jewish and christian telling of a new divine-human relationship. Yet is conserves also the orientation to a covenant people and a tradition which links the present to the creation of the world and which anticipates the fulfillment of a new order under the divine promises.

Genesis, for example is historicized fiction. A Sarah, a Rebecca, an Abraham and Jacob (et al.), may have existed. Some events may have occurred as described in Genesis. But the casting of the characters and the recounting of the journeys of faith from Haran to Canaan, Canaan to Egypt and back, are formed essentially out of the "matter" of many experiences and recurring life patterns. Various literary conventions, such as the wife-sister and betrothal scenes, are used within the framework of a new narrative technique in which we encounter " ... the indeterminacy, the shifting causal concatenations, the ambiguities of a fiction made to resemble the uncertainties of life in history." (Alter: 27) It is fiction as history, fiction thinking out and grounding the historicity of a people providentially led.

On the other hand, many stories are centered in or oriented to historical events and persons. The story of David is a good case in point. After David commits adultery with Bathsheba, he has Uriah slain in battle, and the couple lose the child of their union (II Sam 11-12). There is no reason to doubt that something like these occurrences took place. But the author has shaped his sources to his own end. Not only must he have filled in the gaps of what only the historical persons could have known, but he formed the tale according to his own theological agenda, which is expressed through the appearance of the prophet Nathan with his parable of judgment,

33

then through the ensuing, skillfully related events leading up to the birth of Solomon. After the death of the first infant, the account continues:

> And David comforted Bathsheba his wife and went in to her and lay with her and she gave birth to a son and he called his name Solomon. And Yahweh loved him. And He sent by the hand of Nathan the prophet and called his name Yedidiah for Yahweh's sake. [II Sam 12.24-25][7]

Now Solomon actually became David's successor. It is highly probable that the narrator adumbrates the significance of this eventual fait accompli by briefly but effectively noting the divine favor which rested on Solomon. How could the narrator know that Yahweh loved Solomon? Here as elsewhere the narrator assumes the standpoint of God. One may postulate that the author who gives us the narrator knew Solomon was David's successor. One may add that in any event it is a matter of faith to affirm the divine guidance of a man and a nation; but however one deals with these verses, the fact remains that they are fictional - they are formed by narrative art out of a network of historical events and the convictions of the implied author (on implied author, see note 12 of this chapter). They relate a paradigmatic moment in a fictionalized history.

Although there are mythical and legendary elements within Scripture, understanding biblical narrative neither as myth nor as legend enables us to establish the relation of Israel's historicity to Israel's prose fiction as one whose constant is change, i.e., openness, movement away from closure, revision, characters and events on boundaries. This understanding also aids in the task of using the literary approach as a doorway to theological interpretation (see esp. ch. V, C.).

C. Method of Reading

1. Reading

Every critic owes the reader an indication of how he or she reads the texts in question. Nothing substitutes, of course, for actually doing the reading, but an indication is in order. The word "indication" is used deliberately, for an explanation of a systematic sort would go too far, implying that critical reading is a science which is either esoteric or whose results could be duplicated if one had the right research tools. Just as the critic is engaged in an exploration which may be drudgery at times, but which entices him with the lure of new worlds to discover, so the reader of the critic should expect no more and no less than guidelines or signposts as to what the critic is about.

Even though I engage in technical analysis at points, nothing esoteric is intended in my reading of the relevant texts. The avoidance of pseudoscientific esotericism is one of the reasons why I eschew structuralism as a methodology. I have learned much from structural perspectives, which lead to interesting questions. Structural approaches have helped me look for dipolar oppositions in human speaking and thinking, cultural "codes" as manifest in certain conventions, and underlying transformational ideas (see Williams, 1978, 1980a, 1980b). But much of structuralist analysis is little concerned with the written text and the historicity or existential concerns of authors. If historicism has translated the biblical corpus into a corpse for the sake of sources, sequences, and situations in life (the Sitze im Leben of form criticism), structuralism turns corpus into corpse for the sake of a quasi-mathematical conceptuality.

What is here meant by "method of reading" is the way in which certain questions are asked to make literary and religious sense of the text. Most dictionaries give a range of meanings for "read," from silent scanning of the printed page in order to take in its meaning, to oral recital of written words, to discernment and interpretation. It is, in fact, an interesting word, stemming from the old english "rǣdan," cognate to the old high german "rātan," advise.[8] It has taken on the meaning of understanding and even foretelling in certain contexts (read one's fortune/future). Method of reading here indicates the kinds of questions asked, the kinds of things I am looking for. The implication is that I am "advising" the reader to look and question with me, but advice can be accepted fully, partially, or not at all.

Three principal rubrics stand out in my method of reading: key words, speeches (dialogue, reporting and reported speech), and recurring events (especially typic scenes). These are modified forms of three of the rubrics suggested by Alter (179-85).[9] They will now be taken up in order.

2. Key Words

Key words have long been recognized in biblical scholarship for their function in puns, irony, and various dramatic connections (Wolff; Fishbane; Fokkelman; Williams, 1978;

Alter). Such words are not isolated verbal signs, but rather extend themselves, casting out lines ahead and behind in given stories. Martin Buber and Franz Rosenzweig called this the "Leitwortstil" (lit. "leading" or "guiding word style"). A "Leitwort" as defined by Buber is a word or word-root in a text or related texts whose repetitions suggest the meaning of the text or enhance the meaning. The repetition is even richer if different words from the same root are used because the interplay of sound combinations results in a kind of movement.

... If one imagines the entire text deployed before him, one can sense waves moving back and forth between the words. The measured repetition that matches the inner rhythm of the text, or rather that wells up from it, is one of the most powerful means for conveying meaning without expressing it.[10]

To refer to the Jacob story once again, we note the following instances of the "Leitwortstil." Jacob the younger brother (ṣāᶜîr, Gen 25.23) serves Laban seven years for Rachel the younger daughter (ṣeᶜîrâ, 29.26), but he discovers the morning after the nuptials that Leah the older daughter (beкîrâ, 29.26) was slipped into his tent. Previously Jacob had in opportune fashion gained the birthright (beкōrâ) from his older brother (25.29-34). Jacob also stole the patriarchal blessing (berākâ) from Esau (27.1-29). In his flight from Esau to Haran, when he stops at the place where he has his revelatory dream, his God promises that the land of Canaan will belong to him and his descendants, and that all the clans of the earth will be blessed (nibreкû) through him (28.14). After his long sojourn with the Arameans he returns to Canaan, but before re-entering the land he encounters a mysterious adversary who blesses him (wayebārek ʔōtô) and gives him a name (32.23-31). Thereupon he meets Esau and gives him a gift/blessing ("berākâ" in 33.11, "minḥâ" in 33.10). There are other key words in the Jacob story ("pānîm" [face] and "ᶜābad" [serve] are especially important), but these instances suffice to make the point. If we were to add the words which are not from the same root but are similar in sound (see Williams, 1978: 248-51), we would further bolster Buber's insight regarding the connection of key words, rhythm, and meaning. The irony of divine providence working through the history of Jacob is not, from the standpoint of literary criticism, an abstract theme. "It is a reality con-

cretely embodied in the sight and sound of the text ...."
(Williams, 1978: 251).

3. Speeches: Dialogue, Reporting and Reported Speech

There is no doubt that the <u>word</u> - language and conversation - is of central importance in both scriptural narrative
and wisdom (on the latter, see Williams, 1981: 21-22, 24-26).
Alter may be right when he avers, "Everything in the world of
biblical narrative ultimately gravitates toward dialogue ...."
(182). The exercise of the capacity of speech shows that man
was made, however imperfectly, in the image of God (ibid.).
Alter generalizes that usually "when a narrative event in the
Bible seems important, the writer will render it mainly
through dialogue ...." (ibid.).

At this juncture it is not necessary to argue whether or not
Alter is correct in the radicality of his claim. Suffice it to
observe that when characters speak, the reader should pay
close attention. Among the questions to ask are the following:
when and how does a personage reveal herself through
speech? What does she say in the first reported speech? (This
may be especially revealing.) If a character speaks in some
scenes and not in others, why is this? Why are some episodes
narrated rapidly, while others are described through what an
interlocutor says? If speeches are repeated - for example, if
A gives a message to B who reports it to C -, are there any
changes that might be significant?

A few instances of the significance of dialogue will be
given here, with the full discussion reserved for later
chapters. In Gen 3.2-3 the woman quotes Yahweh Elohim's
prohibition (2.16) in response to the serpent:

> Of the fruits of the trees of the garden we may eat; but
> of the fruit of the tree in the middle of the garden, God
> said, "You shall not eat [plural] any of it nor shall you
> touch [plural] it, lest you die" [plural].

Although the woman was created after God gave the
prohibition, her verbs are in the plural, whereas the decree in
2.16 is in the singular. It is as though she was already there.
With respect to the prohibition itself, the woman adds a
clause to what the deity said, "nor shall you touch it." What
does this suggest? In any case, the first time the woman
speaks she is revealed as one who views herself as addressed
by God when he first spoke to Adam, and she adds words to
the prohibition which reinforce its absoluteness.

In the "typic scenes," which will be discussed at length in the next chapter, there are scenes in which the female says nothing and others in which she is not only the initiator, but is quite aggressive in speaking. In the wife-sister and two of the three betrothal scenes the woman has no part in narrated speech (Gen 12.10-20; 20;[11] 26.1-11, 24; 29.1-20; Ex 2.15-21), whereas she initiates dialogue in two of the three contest scenes (Gen 16.1-6; 29.31-30.24). She has the longest speeches, both interior and exterior, in the third contest scene (I Sam 1). In all save one of the promise or annunciation vignettes she has much to say (Gen 18.1-15; Ju 13.2-24: II Kings 4.8-17; Lk 1.5-25 is the exception). Why the difference concerning the woman's part in dialogue among these kinds of typic scene? Sarai for example - she is completely silent while she is played as a pawn between Abram and the pharaoh in Gen 12. She first speaks in Gen 16 when she knows that she is unable to become pregnant. This is the beginning of the agon or contest with Hagar. That she first speaks at this juncture discloses something essential about her role in the story of Israel's origins. She states at the beginning of the episode that Yahweh has prevented her from childbearing, so Abram is to have sexual relations with her maidservant Hagar. Sarai says,

Perhaps I shall be built up through her. [16.2]

In Abraham's response to the king of Gerar, Gen 20.11-13, he presents two matters that neither he nor God has previously stated, nor the narrator reported.

And moreover, she is indeed my sister, my father's daughter she is, but not my mother's. And she became my wife. Now it happened that as God made me wander from my father's house I said to her, "This is the favor that you will do for me: at every place we enter say of me, 'He is my brother.'" [vv. 12-13]

This is the first time the reader is informed of Abraham's request that Sarah assume the guise of sister everywhere they sojourn. Even more striking is the news that she is indeed his half-sister! Does the writer indicate something of importance in a speech laden with new information?

One more matter concerning speeches. Robert Polzin, following V. N. Voloshinov (= M. Bakhtin), has recently made the distinction between "reporting" and "reported" speech a methological principle in his interpretation of Deuteronomy and the deuteronomic history (Polzin, 1980: 18-19 and passim). In reporting speech a persona reports or narrates something within the narrative. In other words, it is not dialogue, but a shorter or longer report, description, or narration that the narrator allows a character to present. Reported speech is the quotation of someone within reporting speech. In Deuteronomy the narrator presents Moses as speaker. Moses tells the story (reporting speech), but in a few instances (about 56 verses) he quotes God directly. This distinction is valuable as a way of getting at the different perspectives and voices of a work, as well as contributing to an assessment of the writer's or text's own view of given figures. For instance, in Deuteronomy Moses is so important that he tells the story of Israel's journey to the Transjordan, and it is he who knows the words of Yahweh. Yahweh addresses the people only in the decalogue, 5.6-21, and even then it is Moses who quotes the divine words. But if it is only Moses who knows what God says and intends, it is the narrator who knows what Moses says. The narrator is the mouthpiece of Moses, who in turn is God's spokesman. How reliable is the narrator? What kind of implied author[12] is it who makes such grand (implied) claims for himself through the narrator, who pretends to know Moses' words, who claims to see from God's point of view?

The distinction between reported and reported speech will not assume the basic methodological importance in this study that it has for Polzin, but it is a valuable way of looking at the woman's general social status in the stories. Not that her social status is equivalent to her religious significance. In fact, it may be that her limited social and political power increases her availability as a metaphor of Israel in the world. At any rate, to anticipate some of our results, we frequently find feminine figures speaking, but seldom do they narrate a story, and when they do it is usually very brief. To narrate significant happenings to others presupposes a measure of authority - unless the text itself raises a question in reporting that someone in the story narrates something. The exceptions to this pattern are Hannah, Deborah, Judith, and Mary. (See Hannah's prayer, I Sam 2.1-10, Deborah's song, Ju 5, Judith's song of thanksgiving, Judith 16.2-17, and Mary's "magnificat," Lk 1.46-55).

4. Recurring Events

The recurrence of events is one of the hallmarks of biblical style. "Recurrence" is not intended to suggest the repetition of exactly the same thing; there is repetition of situations and conventional scenes, but there are always variations and different nuances that flow into the narrative movement and provide a good part of the interweaving of continuity and change.

The two principal kinds of recurring events are the repetition of basically the same event and different versions of the same event. Only the former is pertinent to this book. It is, in my terminology, the "typic scene" (Williams, 1980a; Alter, ch. 3).[13] The typic scene is a convention of story telling. Like conventions in painting and iconography, it has fixed elements that constrain the artist to work within them. For the artist there is a social necessity to offer the continuity of the long standing convention that the audience expects. The challenge to creativity is to achieve new meaning by dropping or adding an element here and there (too much dropping or adding would ruin the continuity), to effect different nuances, or to mold variations on the traditional elements. A deviation from this pattern of making changes or new nuances within a framework of continuity represents a fundamentally new vision of the subject, and would reflect either an iconoclastic author or an audience that has already accepted basic changes in its perceptions of reality. An example of new vision to be presented later in the book is the book of Ruth. The author of Ruth employs the convention of the betrothal, or maiden at the well (see Alter: ch. 3; Culley: 41-43), but exactly reverses its constituent elements.

The typic scene of the betrothal is instructive for giving an idea of such scenes. There are three betrothal scenes, Gen 24.10-61; 29.1-20; Ex 2.15-21. The basic elements of the convention:

1. Hero traveling to a foreign land
2. Hero stopping at a well in the foreign land
3. Maiden coming to the well
4. Hero acting on maiden's behalf, showing exceptional strength or ability
5. Maiden running home to report what has occurred
6. Stranger-hero being invited into maiden's household
7. Hero marrying maiden at the well

There are several variations among the scenes:

Element 1. In Gen 24 it is not the hero (patriarch), but his servant who seeks a wife for the patriarch's son. In Gen 29 and Ex 2 the hero has fled from his own land in order to escape a vengeful male.

Element 3. Maidens (plural) at the well in Ex 2.

Element 4. The traveler does not perform a great feat in Gen 24, but God grants a sign enabling him to fulfill his mission (vv. 14, 18).

Element 7. In Gen 24 the servant takes the maiden back to his homeland for his master's son.

As already stated, the book of Ruth employs this convention by way of reversal. The convention is also employed in John 4, with frequently ironic variations which are in keeping with John's christology. (Williams, 1980a: 113-14)

The historico-genetic theses of source, form and redaction critics have been generally wrong about the typic scenes. Once the literary convention is recognized, there can be little basis for asserting an "original" version of which the other scenes are variants. (See the similar statement of Culley: 39-40.) Whether or not different story tellers have shaped typic scenes is a difficult question. Some of them, for example the wife-sister scene in Gen 12, 20 and 26, may well come from the same author.

In short, and as already stated, although historical knowledge or theory is the necessary condition of literary interpretation (see above, B.2.), the aesthetic and religious values of the text will unfold for the reader only if the reader discerns the role of ancient literary conventions.

Chapter II

THE ARCHE-MOTHER:
THE MOTHER OF ISRAEL'S BEGINNINGS

KERÉNYI has said that mythology is characterized by a narrative return to origins. At a profound level it does not deal with the "aition," the reason or cause of things, but with the first principle, the archē. "Behind the 'Why?' stands the 'Whence?,' behind the 'aition' the 'archē' " (7). Biblical narrative as a mode of thinking obviously refers to origins in the story of the beginnings of the world and of Israel; yet its "archai" are always the beginnings as intersecting the present, as open to the vicissitudes of historical existence under God who is Presence.

There is a great difference between the prose fiction of ancient israelite literature and the myths and epics of the ancient world, even though they both are concerned with the "archē," or in hebrew, the "rē?šît" (see Vawter). The babylonian Enuma Elish moves through the commingling of opposites to the clash of the younger and older gods, climaxing in the triumph of Marduk over the goddess of the salt waters, Tiamat, and ending with the establishment of the great sanctuary Babylon and the praise of Marduk. It comes to a closure; it does not open up to a further story of Marduk and his people. The epic of Gilgamesh raises questions about this mythological world, especially man's fate of death vis-à-vis the immortality of the gods. When Gilgamesh returns to his city after a futile quest (although he is much wiser), there is not the same closure as in the cosmogony because the ending implies the value of further human projects in the city. Yet there is an essential resignation to the fate of man in the city where Ishtar, in spite of his attempt to reject the controls she imposes (tablet 6), is the victor after all (end of tablet 11).

In spite of these differences between biblical prose fiction and the mythic mode of expression, Kerényi's distinction between cause and principle is useful, and it suggests a way of viewing the first feminine subject of this study: as the arche-mother. "Matriarch" is a word now tied to Sarah, Rebecca and Rachel in Genesis. I have in mind not only the ancestresses but also the women who function similarly in the stories of Israel's genesis and destiny. These are specifically the tales of Sarah, Rebecca, Rachel, Moses's mother and the pharaoh's daughter, Zipporah, Samson's mother, and Hannah. The tale of the prophet and the woman of Shunem in I Kings 4.8-37 bears an interesting relation to the stories of the arche-mother, although she is not important in the recounting of origins.

Many of the mother tales are told in typic scenes. As already pointed out, the typic scenes are conventions of ancient israelite literary art. Much as in our Hollywood westerns or medieval iconography of the annunciation to Mary (both examples used by Alter: 48-49, 51), there are predetermined elements that the narrator must employ in the convention which, by its very use, already signals the idea that something typical and thus important about Israel past and present is being related.[1] Yet the predetermined elements are manipulated and modeled in keeping with the technique of narrative as process.

But the typic scenes do not exhaust the repertory of mother stories. I shall not attempt a rehearsal of the relevant gamut of narratives, but two other significant features of the texts will be highlighted: the mother as mediating agent and the disappearance of the mother. The remainder of the chapter will, then, be devoted to four topics: four kinds of typic scenes, the mother as mediating agent, the disappearance of the mother, and a concluding set of summary reflections on the arche-mother and narrative thinking.

A. The Typic Scenes

The elements of the betrothal scene have already been indicated (ch. I, C.4.). Since the first two passages, Gen 24.10-61 and 29.1-19 stem from the narrative theme of the need to marry within the larger family, the third one, Ex 2.15-21, may presuppose the same theme. The Midianites were descendants of Abraham according to Gen 25.2. In each case the bride to be is found at a well, and in all instances the meeting is fraught with dramatic tension.

The Rebecca segment centers on the fine qualities of Rebecca and something that is absent: the action of Isaac. Isaac is passive, everything is done for him. After the servant brings Rebecca to him we learn that he takes Rebecca into his deceased mother's tent and is comforted "after the death of his mother" (24.67). Isaac is borne by Sarah, a source of laughing/rejoicing for her (yiṣḥāq, "he laughs, plays"); he is taken by his father Abraham at God's command to be offered as a sacrifice to the God of the mysterious journey; and now a wife is found for him among his uncle's children, one who replaces his mother. Later on, ch. 27, as he lies on his death bed, he is deceived by Rebecca and Jacob into blessing Jacob rather than Esau. His blindness in old age (27.1) is a fitting image of his ignorance of what has happened to him throughout his life.

As for Rebecca, she is depicted as a lovely and hospitable virgin maiden. The repetition and lengthy speeches in this typic scene lead up to her family's blessing on her:

O you our sister, be the mother of myriads, and may your children possess the gates of their enemies. [24.60]

With this blessing the narrator quietly moves Rebecca into the cycle of God's promises to the patriarchs (Gen 12.1-3; 15.5; passim). By contrast to the servant's frequent dialogue and one lengthy speech (vv. 33-49), Rebecca says only what is necessary, but her words are dramatically telling. At the well she tells the servant to drink and then offers to water his camels also (vv. 18-19). The servant reviews at length his mandate, which includes new information: he will be accursed if he does not fulfill his mission! Then feasting and negotiations take place. After all this the mother and brother ask her whether she will go with the man.

And she said, "I will go." [v. 58]

Later, as the servant and Rebecca approach the habitation of Abraham in the Negev, she sees Isaac.

And Rebecca lifted her eyes [cf. Gen 22.4, 13] and she saw Isaac and she dismounted from the camel and she said to the servant, "Who is this man coming in the field to meet us?" And the servant said, "It is my master." And she took the veil and covered herself. [vv. 64-65]

From her few lines of dialogue we learn that Rebecca is lovely, helpful and able, modest, and above all ready to go on the journey to a new land and to a husband related to her, but whom neither she nor her family had met.

In the Rachel episode Rachel is completely silent and is

relatively inactive in contrast to Jacob, who dominates the scene. He rolls a large stone from the mouth of the well, one which evidently usually required more than one man to budge (see the third person plural, gāl^{e}lû, "they have rolled," in 29.8). The connection of his sighting of Rachel with his act of rolling the stone intimates that Jacob is inspired by what he sees and is showing off a bit. But we learn something about Rachel, too. The unobtrusive narrator lets us know that she is a shepherdess - she works with sheep, as does Jacob, a sign of the divinely favored person in the Bible (Abel, Isaac, Jacob, Joseph, Moses, David). She is beautiful, as are all the matriarchs. She is Jacob's cousin, the daughter of Laban, his mother's brother. Nonetheless, Rachel is given nothing to say. She does not speak until the beginning of the contest scene: "Give me children, otherwise I am as good as dead" (30.1).

The Exodus scene presents seven daughters of the "priest of Midian." The terse rapidity of the action as well as the anonymity of the daughters are features of a narrative skill that brings together the customary elements in great economy. The narrator can do this in part because his audience would be less interested in Moses's future wife than in the ancestresses of Genesis. This focus on Moses is stressed in the report of the daughters to Reuel:

> And they said, "An egyptian man rescued us from the shepherds and moreover he even drew water for us and watered the flock. [2.19]

The rendering, "he even drew water for us," is an attempt to express the emphasis in hebrew (dālōh dālâ, lit. "to draw he drew up"). Moses's ability and kindness are highlighted. There is also a possible allusion to the rescue of Moses - his being drawn up - from the river by the egyptian princess (Ex 2.5-10) and to his future function as the leader who would guide Israel through the waters. Such allusions are not necessarily of theological significance, but the web of associations is both entertaining and a continual reminder of symbolic meanings to the knowledgable audience.[2] Finally, since the reader and hearer, knowing the larger narrative context, think of Moses as a Hebrew, it is an eye-opener to hear him described as an Egyptian. It would have been easy for the author to omit "miṣrî," "Egyptian," whether we envision the author as master of the larger Torah story or imagine a story-teller orally relating a brief tale. The audience is reminded of Moses's egyptian acculturation, which alludes both to his having been rescued by the princess and his future charismatic role vis-à-vis the Egyptians.

Summarily stated, the only active role of the arche-mother in the betrothal scenes is to hurry home to report the appearance of the male protagonist at the well, although Rebecca's small share in the dialogue is dramatically sig-nificant. The hero performs an extraordinary deed (in Gen 24 a providential sign is given), and that it occurs at the well where he meets the lovely maiden is probably a narrative signal that the soon to be married couple and their progeny are divinely blessed, thus they will be successful and fertile (see Alter: 52).

The wife-sister scenes feature Sarah and Rebecca (Gen 12.10-20; 20; 26.1-14). The standard elements:

1. Famine in Canaan.
2. Patriarch and family travel to foreign land.
3. Patriarch lies about wife, presenting her as his sister.
4. The wife is taken for the royal harem.
5. Divine intervention.
6. King demands explanation.
7. Benefits conferred upon patriarch.

The variations:

Element 1. In Gen 20 famine is not mentioned as the reason for the sojourn. The journey is commanded by Yahweh in Gen 20.
Element 3. The wife turns out actually to be the patriarch's half-sister in Gen 26.
Element 4. Wife not taken into the royal harem in Gen 26.
Element 5. No divine intervention to avert disastrous con-sequences in Gen 26, although the promise of divine pro-tection is given in the revelation at the beginning of the episode (v. 2).

Again, as in the betrothal scenes, the ancestresses are prized objects in the complex interweaving of chance events and divine design that lead Israel on destiny's way. They have no part in direct dialogue. Sarah is reported as speaking once (20.5), but here as in the other passages it is a matter of lying for the patriarch's sake. The status of the woman as an object viewed impersonally is especially striking in Gen 12.10-20, where Sarai is identified by name only twice, and in both instances her status as wife of Abraham is immediately indicated by apposition (vv. 11, 17). She is twice called "hā?iššâ" - "the woman" - (vv. 14 and 15), and a possessive pronoun (his, my, your) is attached to "?iššâ" five times.

Still, if the matriarch is passive and treated as an object, her importance in the scene and in the larger story is clear. Without the matriarch the promises to Abraham are endangered. Abraham (and later Isaac) must have a male descendant through the right woman. Moreover, there is barely concealed here, especially in Gen 12, the awareness that Israel without God's aid might have been sired by a foreign father. On the other hand, the welfare of the foreign kings and their subjects is threatened in turn due to this breach in the continuity of the promised destiny. Indeed, a mythical element enters into the Gerar scene. We are told by the narrator, in a gentle reminder of his omniscience, "For Yahweh had completely closed all the wombs of the house of Abimelech" (20.18). The taking of the arche-mother had resulted in the infertility of the king's women.

In the two Sarah scenes the arche-mother is desired by foreigners for her beauty. Rebecca's beauty is introduced in the betrothal scene prior to the wife-sister episode. The arche-mother's beauty is a code communicating that she is blessed and that her progeny will be favored. This seems to work out almost without exception for biblical persons (Sarah, Rebecca, Rachel, Joseph, David, Bathsheba, Judith, Esther).[3]

That the patriarch passes off his wife as his sister touches on an interesting problem in interpretation. We have already noted (ch. I, B.2.) the once dominant thesis in biblical scholarship that the wife as sister obliquely reflected ancestral practices during the bronze age. This position is now discredited by the research of cuneiform scholars, but if the wife-sister theme is not in any sense a historical datum, how should it be construed? I have argued that it should be construed as a literary archetype, one indeed with mythical roots but which functions dramatically in Gen 12 and 20 as a representation of the sense of crisis attending the narrator's depiction of Israel's origins. This feeling of the tenuousness of Israel in history must have evoked a sympathetic hearing during and after the babyonian exile.

The crisis is presented in the form of placing the ancestress in a compromising situation which involved her in the possibility, if not the actuality, of forbidden sexual relations with a foreign king or with the ancestor. Although the narrator passes over it quietly, the train of events in Gen

12 seems to come about because Sarai is forced into adultery (see Polzin: 1975). In Gen 20 it is apparent that there is no sexual contact between Sarah and the king, but then we learn that she is really Abraham's half-sister. The latter narrative fact is revealed to us as rather a surprise in Abraham's speech, 20.11-13. The audience is not prepared at all for this turn of events.

Whatever the age of the Gerar episode in its final form, the ancient israelite audience would have presumably viewed the marriage of brother and sister as incest (Lev 18.9; 20.17). The sexual purity laws were generally known and accepted long before the babylonian exile, so the non-observance of them by the ancestors could have been offensive to many Israelites - unless the wife-sister convention carried with it an archetypal theme that was known or felt to be important enough to allow the waiving of the usual requirements for ancestors and heroes.

This deeper theme has to do with Israel's origins. The actual and apparent adultery imposed on Sarah in Gen 12 and 20 could have led to the nonexistence of Israel. The foreign ruler, the kings of Egypt and Gerar, becomes the narrative embodiment of this threat. As to Sarah as half-sister of Abraham, this probably functions in a manner similar to the theme of incest and close family relationships in the mating of gods and heroes (see Williams, 1980a: 116-17 and nn. 21-22). A universal value is suggested that the biblical stories share in their own fashion: the closeness of the primordial mother and father. Those from whom the people of the tradition are descended are not "foreign" to each other but are related; they are of "one flesh." The descendants come from one, from one origin rather than from many (i.e., from those who are foreign to one another). Thus is accomplished a symbolic representation of Israel's one origin and destiny in a world of danger and conflict.[4]

In the next two typic scenes to be considered the arche-mothers are presented in a different light. These are the contest of the barren wife and the promise to the barren wife. The elements of the contest of the barren wife (Gen 16.1-6 and 21.1-7; 29.31-30.24; I Sam 1).

1. The favored wife is barren.
2. The husband has another woman who is a rival.
3. The rival woman is fertile, bears a son for the husband.
4. Rival woman belittles the barren wife, bringing about the conflict.

5. The barren wife is eventually heard by God, has a son.

The variations:
Element 2. The rivals are sisters in Gen 29.31ff.
Element 3. In Gen 29.31ff. the rival wife, Leah, does not belittle Rachel, although there may be a triumphant note in the litany of the naming of the first four sons. 29.31-35.
Element 5. Sarah does not have her son until 21.1-7, after the Gerar episode. It should be noted also that she is the only one who has the rival woman expelled, and this woman is a servant and foreigner (Egyptian).

In the agon or contest the arche-mother takes the initiative as she does in no other typic scene. She initiates the process whereby she overcomes the shame of her condition and the vexation caused by her rival.

The brief scene in Gen 16.1-6 is indicative of this female vitality. At the human level Sarai is completely in charge. The ultimate subject in the situation is, of course, Yahweh, as Sarai avers (v. 2). Her statement to Abram, "Look here, Yahweh has prevented me (^{c}așaranî) from giving birth" (v. 2), reads like a subtle narrative anticipation of 20.18. The verb "^{c}āṣar," to close, seal up, is used in both accounts. As Sarai had been barren until she and Abram received their new names, the promise of Yahweh was reaffirmed, and the regal status of the couple was revealed, so anyone who tries to take her will lose fertility. Only Yahweh can "enclose her," foreign powers cannot.

The status of Sarai in Gen 16 is revealed in the use of her personal name, which occurs seven times in six verses. She also initiates the dialogue - and has her rival expelled.

The rival, Hagar, is interesting in her own right. As an Egyptian she is a living reminder of the sojourn in Egypt in Gen 12. It is thus ironic that Sarai would give her to Abram,in order to be "built up" through her. Having a son by Hagar, even though Sarai could lay claim to maternal rights, would leave Abram and Sarai in the situation of establishing a family tree through an Egyptian!

The narrator performs the difficult task of treating Hagar sympathetically, acknowledging the harshness in Sarai's action of having her expelled ("And Sarai afflicted her," 16.6), while communicating the necessity of Sarai's act from the viewpoint of narrative omniscience. There is a certain necessity in the course of events which overrides everything else, but nonetheless due recognition is given to human needs and emotions.

Hagar, in fact, is the subject of two episodes that may be typic scenes in 16.7-16 and 21.8-21. There are only two such tales, but they have in common expulsion into the wilderness, divine revelation, naming of the son, and the divine promise that he will be the ancestor of a great nation. Hagar is driven into the wilderness and Ishmael is associated with <u>wildness</u> (16.12); this image of the wild coupled with Abraham as the father points to Hagar and her descendants as related to, yet opposing the reality of Israel. She is an image of another <u>order</u>, a counter-order that is not enfolded into the tradition but whose importance and relation to Israel is affirmed. We shall look at her again in the fourth chapter.

The struggle between Rachel and Leah in 29.31-30.24 portrays vividly both the power of the matriarch in some spheres of life and the limitations placed upon her. The sisters have most of the dialogue, which consists primarily of naming their sons and interpreting the names. On the other hand, they are fighting over a man, Jacob, in order to have his sons, and the name of the daughter, Dinah, receives no comment (30.21). In spite of the power that may be implied in the right of naming, thus of seeking to determine the child's destiny, the dialogue proceeds in a comic-ironic vein which may make it difficult for the audience to take the women seriously. When it is clear that Rachel is losing out as Leah bears Reuben, Simon, Levi and Judah in rapid succession, Rachel gives Jacob her maid Bilhah, "that I may be built up through her" (30.3; cf. 16.2). Bilhah bears a son.

And Rachel said, "God has judged me (dānnanî) and indeed heard my voice, and has given me a son." Therefore she called him name Dan. [30.6]

Bilhah gives birth again (30.8):

And Rachel said, "Godly wrestlings (naptûlê ʔelōhîm) have I wrestled (niptaltî) with my sister, and I have prevailed" [cf. 32.29]. And she called his name Naftali.

But Leah does not take this lying down. When she sees that she is no longer having children, she gives her maid Zilpah to Jacob. Zilpah bears a son. Leah says, "Fortune (gād) is come!" (v. 11) So he is named Gad. And Zilpah gives her another son. Leah says (v. 13):

Am I happy (beʔāsrî), for the women will call me happy!

So this one is named Asher.

It should be said, however, that Jacob hardly appears more noble that the sisters, and in fact is a rather helpless schmuck, both in his initial exasperation with Rachel (30.2) and especially in being hired out by Rachel to Leah in exchange for some mandrakes (dûdā?îm, reputedly aphrodisiacal) that Reuben found (30.14-18). From this union Leah conceives and has a son, Issachar, saying, "God has given me my hire" (śᵉkārî, 30.18).

But Rachel is finally able to conceive, and the narrative signals to us that this is the most significant son. Rachel is given two comments that enframe the son's name, Joseph (30.23-24). Both of Rachel's remarks play on the name of Joseph. After she conceives and bears a son she says, "God has removed (?āsap) my reproach."

> And she called his name Joseph [yôsēp], saying, "Yahweh add [yōsēp] to me another son."

The sense of Rachel's comments is doubly interesting in that it may be taken to mean the coincidence of opposites in Joseph. He is associated both with removing (here, Rachel's dishonor) and adding (here, the increase of Rachel's progeny). As the primary actor of the concluding segment of Genesis (chs. 37, 39-50) who provides a dramatic bridge from the ancestors to Moses and the exodus (Coats), Joseph embodies many traits of both the patriarchs and the matriarchs (Williams, 1979).

Meanwhile, Rachel may have sealed her fate in this agon scene. The first words that we hear from her, in this typic scene as well as in Genesis, are words of frustration that Jacob perceives as bordering on the sacrilegious.

> And she said to Jacob, "Give me children lest I die!" And Jacob became furious with Rachel and he said, "Am I in God's place who has withheld from you the fruit of the womb?" [30.1-2]

At the end of the scene when she bears Joseph, she names him with a wish for another son. This is exactly what occurs - she has another son, but she dies in childbirth (35.18).

Though we know from the betrothal and wife-sister scenes that the arche-mother is divinely favored, the narrator injects further suspense into the story of origins by using the typic agon scene. We know that the outcome will be a happy one, as did the ancient readers and hearers. But this

51

knowledge does not annul enjoyment of the conflicts in the course of the events and the reactions of different characters.

The mother is in conflict with a rival, who is now closely related (Rachel and Leah), now not related at all (Hannah and Penninah), and in one case even a foreigner (Sarah and Hagar). She engages in aggressive action in order to establish herself, and finally she does bear a son because God grants him to her. She struggles, but her efforts would avail nothing unless the deity opened her womb.

The promise scenes show the heroine as likewise active, though not in the same way and to the same extent as in the contest tableaus. The elements of the scene (Gen 18.1-15; Ju 13.2-24; II Kgs 4.8-17; Lk 1.5-25):

1. The wife is barren.
2. A messenger from the God appears to the woman.
3. The messenger promises a son.
4. The event is confirmed in spite of human doubt.
5. The promised son is born and given a significant name.

The variations:

Element 2. There are many variations on this element. In Gen 18 three "men" come to Abraham's tent, one of whom turns out to be Yahweh. The other two are presumably angels or other members of "benê ʾelōhîm," "sons of God" in the heavenly court. The promise is announced to Abraham, but Sarah overhears it. In Ju 13 the messenger appears twice to the woman, who brings her husband to see him when the second hierophany occurs. This messenger takes the form of a man, but is referred to as "God" in v. 22. In II Kings 4 the prophet Elisha is the messenger. Luke's scene presents the husband as the recipient of the announcement.

Element 5. The name of the son is not given in II Kings 4. This is in keeping with the intention of the prophetic legends to display the power and authority of the prophet. The identity of the parents is thus of no concern in the tale.

Gen 18.1-15 is a finely wrought combination of typical human occurrences, depiction of character, and divine visitation that bespeaks the extraordinary working of providence within life's routines and age-old problems. We are told at the beginning that Yahweh appeared to Abraham by the terebinth of Mamre. The narrator clues us in, so we are reminded of his omniscience, though the opening notice is so quick and unobtrusive that the domesticity of the ensuing scene is not overwhelmed. The ordinary routine of seminomadic existence is indicated right away: Abraham sits in the door of his tent during the heat of the day. He welcomes the visitors and has Sarah and a servant prepare a feast, not failing himself to participate in the required work. The visitors eat, and from this point the dialogue is deserving of full quotation (vv. 9-15):

> And they said to him, "Where is Sarah your wife." And he said, "In the tent." And he said, "I will certainly return to you in the spring, and lo, Sarah your wife shall have a son." And Sarah heard in the tent door, which was behind him. (And Abraham and Sarah were old, well along in years. Sarah had ceased to have menstrual periods.) And Sarah laughed [wattiṣḥaq] to herself, saying, "After not having had pleasure, and my husband is old?" And Yahweh said to Abraham, "Why did Sarah laugh [ṣāḥᵃqâ], saying, 'Am I indeed to bear a child and I have become old?' At the set time I will come back to you in the spring and Sarah shall have a son." And Sarah denied it - "I didn't laugh" [ṣāḥaqtî], for she was afraid. "No, but you did laugh" [ṣāḥāqt].

One can hardly imagine a scene that bears so greatly the stamp of ancient folklore while exhibiting the signs of an author's art. The play on "ṣāḥaq," "laugh, play," so often noted by the exegetes, anticipates the birth of Isaac, in hebrew "yiṣḥāq," "he laughs." In the larger literary context it has at least two connotations. One is that "one laughs," whoever hears about it, in joy over the birth of Isaac to Sarah and Abraham (Gen 21.6-7). And with reference to the promise scene in Gen 18 it suggests that Yahweh has the last laugh.

In the wife-sister convention we have seen the threat of foreign powers, in the agon we have observed the threat posed by the rival woman who is not the true arche-mother. Here in the annunciation scene we find the condition of old age, but it too, like all the other dangers, is resolved by the God who visits the blessed couple. The God comes in human form, as either one of the men or as all three (so von Rad, 1972a: 204-5). The fact of a theophany finally comes home to Sarah and she shows fear, but the total framework mitigates the reaction of awe to the numinous. Furthermore, Yahweh's promise to return is not understood literally in the larger story; the "return" is rather the process of conception and childbirth.

Sarah reacts in a normal manner to what she hears: she laughs to herself. Her laughter simultaneously depicts her as ordinary and independent. How could an old woman who had not menstruated or even had sex for some time bear a child?[5] When she denies that she laughed, the scene ends abruptly with Yahweh's curt rejoinder, "lō? kî ṣāḥāqt," "no, but you did laugh." Are these three words ominous, or do they simply serve to repeat once more the thematic word play?

In Ju 13 and II Kings 4 the barren wife has a more active role than in the other two scenes. The mother of Samson is the one who is visited initially by the angel, and at the end of the episode she reassures her husband that Yahweh had no intention to slay them (13.23). The woman of Shunem often receives Elisha as a guest, and eventually she persuades her husband to build a chamber for him on their roof. This kindness inspires Elisha to promise her a son, who will arrive "in the spring."[6] However, there is no indication in the scene that she wants a son. This will be of consequence in the later story where the son dies and she reproaches Elisha for having caused her grief (4.28).

Alter has pointed out what may be a significant change in a repeated speech reported in Ju 13 (Alter: 101). The messenger tells the woman that the child is to be a nazirite, and he "shall begin to deliver Israel from the power of the Philistines" (v. 5). In reporting this promise to her husband she says nothing about delivering Israel, but states that he "shall be a nazirite of God from the womb to the day of his death" (v. 7). Although "min-habbeṭen ᶜad-yôm môtô" would be a formal, elevated way of saying "all his life," the emphasis has shifted, in nuance at least, from the promise of a great liberator to the promise of a nazirite. The dubious character of Samson's status as a judge and liberator is thus adumbrated. In a similar vein, the mother-to-be omits the angel's injunction that "no razor shall come upon his head' (v. 5). A small detail perhaps, but since the reader knows how Samson meets his fate the omission in the mother's reported speech is probably another signal of Samson's dark destiny.

Luke's use of the typic scene directs the divine message entirely to the father Zechariah. Although Elizabeth is mentioned in the long promise speech, she has no role in the scene until the conclusion, when she says, "The Lord has done this for me now that it has pleased him to remove my reproach among men" (Lk 1.25). Her affirmation is very close to the LXX of Rachel's words in Gen 30.23: "apheilen ho theos mou to oneidos" (cf. I Sam 1.11), "God has removed my re-proach."

Actually, there are two other biblical promise scenes that could be included, Matt 1.18-25 and Lk 1.26-38. The latter is the classical christian source of the annunciation tradition. The only difference in pattern between the gospel scenes and the ancient israelite model is that the woman is not barren, but a young virgin. The young virgin is an image in opposition to the (old?) barren wife. But the opposites meet in that the outcome is the same in both cases: through a wonderful divine providence the religious hero is conceived in a womb brought to conception by no human father. For early Christianity this was one symbolic mode of expressing the transcendent meaning of its salvific revelation-event: the reality of this son is not of human origins, but of God. Nonetheless, apart from the woman's virginity one finds the same elements of the promise convention in the gospel accounts of the annunci-ation to Mary: divine messenger; messenger promises a son; event confirmed in spite of human doubt; promised son is given a significant name.

B. The Arche-Mother As Mediating Agent

The arche-mother often performs a mediating function in the origin stories. The narrated circumstances of these acts vary greatly; some occur in typic scenes, some do not. The mediating act sometimes enables the arche-father or the chosen one (e.g., Moses) to escape some danger and thus to realize his destiny. The danger varies - it may come from a foreign ruler, a relative, or even from God. A common thread in the instances is that the hostile reality is "male." Even though the biblical God is not literally a "male" who is thus sexual and has or seeks a "female," "he" is characteristic-ally portrayed as though he had male traits.[7]

Sarah figures in the wife-sister scenes as a kind of "buffer" protecting the patriarch from danger. It is her beauty, of course, that endangers him in the first place (at least from his standpoint). She both attracts the attention of foreign rulers who desire her and allows herself to be passed off as his sister in order to protect her husband. The audience knows that it is through her that Abraham is to become a great nation, so it is as if he can't live with her and he can't live without her! Moreover, it is on her account that the patriarch prospers in the foreign setting, and in one instance he is recognized as a "prophet" whose intercession with God brings about the restoration of human life and fertility (Gen 20.7, 17).[8]

Sarah takes the initiative in protecting Isaac from having to share his inheritance with Ishmael (Gen 21.8-15). Her demand that Hagar and Ishmael be banished from the clan is severe, and Abraham is very distressed by it (21.11). In fact, the narrator by implication indicates the injustice done by telling us that God spoke at this point to Abraham to reassure him that this was the best thing for the divinely intended destiny of Israel: "... for through Isaac offspring will be named after you" (kî beyiṣḥāq yiqqārēʔ lekā zeraC, 21.12): Sarah thus manages to eliminate the reminder of the egyptian sojourn, Hagar and Hagar's son by Abraham. However, God intends to bless Hagar and Ishmael, too (Gen 16.10; 21.20), and the descendants of Ishmael reappear ironically in the Joseph story (Gen 37.27-28).

As Sarah is the initiator of the action in Gen 16 and 21, so also is Rebecca in Gen 27. Her plot to deceive Isaac and gain the father's blessing for her youngest son completely changes the life situations of Jacob and Esau. The background of the mother's plot is given in Gen 25.19-26. Rebecca sought an oracle of Yahweh when she felt the fetuses struggling within her. The oracle tells her that two peoples are in her womb and that the "older' (rab) would serve the "younger" (ṣāCîr),[9] presumably alluding to Esau and Jacob, respectively. Rebecca favors her younger twin as Isaac favors the older, and she thus conceives the ruse to gain the patriarchal blessing for Jacob.

Rebecca orders Jacob, who is a "smooth" man, to diguise himself in Esau's skins, with kid skins on his hands and neck, and to take the goat meat to his father which will be seasoned to taste like the venison that Esau is wont to bring. The goat skins are necessary because Esau is "hairy" (ṣāCir, 27.11),[10] and so the blind patriarch will be fooled if he feels the skin of the bringer of meat. Jacob apprehensively protests that Father may find him out and curse rather than bless him, but Rebecca replies, "Upon me be your curse, my son, only do what I say and get (them) for me" (27.13). Jacob obeys her and wins the blessing.

Rachel is not a mediating agent for Jacob or her sons in the same unambiguous sense that one finds in the stories of Sarah and Rebecca. However, the comic chase scene in Gen 31 implies that Rachel's theft of Laban's teraphim is an audacious act on behalf of the Jacob clan. When Laban catches up with Jacob and family it is surprising that he says nothing of the livestock that Jacob outwitted him in gaining. The narrative interest does not lie there. The silence on this matter may explain why the narrator gives Laban a speech in which he avows his good intentions and mentions that Jacob's God had spoken to him on Jacob's behalf:

Beware of speaking with Jacob about anything good or evil. [31.29; see v. 24]

But Laban is not sanguine about the loss of the teraphim, images of his guardian gods. Laban vows that whoever committed the theft shall die. Jacob does not know that it is Rachel who has stolen them. Laban searches for his statuettes.

Now Rachel had taken the teraphim and placed them in a camel saddle, and sat upon them. And Laban felt all about the tent, but didn't find them. And Rachel said, "Don't be angry, sir, that I cannot rise before you, but the way of women is upon me." And he searched on, but couldn't find the teraphim. [31.34-35]

The "way of women" (derek nāšîm): Laban thinks it means menstruation, but it is likely to be a pun that the narrator shares with the reader. Rachel's "way" is one that fools Laban and of which Jacob is ignorant, which is reminiscent of the childbearing contest where he is the pawn of Rachel and Leah (esp. 30.15-16).

Whatever the icons were and whatever they represented exactly, Laban is practically beside himself over losing them. In any event, Jacob apparently gains another claim to power over the Aramean just as he obtained the patriarchal blessing rather than Esau.[11]

Three women enable Moses to become the great leader and covenant mediator of the Hebrews. His mother, to save him when the egyptian king commands all newborn hebrew males to be executed, hides him for three months and then places him in an "ark" (tēbâ) in the Nile (Ex 2.3; cf. Gen 6.14, passim). The egyptian princess who takes the baby from the water and raises him is especially interesting. Here Egypt reappears in a positive light, as it does in the Joseph story. Moses is reared as an Egyptian, so that he, like Joseph, becomes culturally an Egyptian. The princess enables Moses to survive in Egypt vis-à-vis her father, the king. He is thus spared for the future good of Israel, a future that will ironically bring her adopted son into conflict with her people.

Finally, when Yahweh seeks to slay Moses as the latter returns to begin his mission in Egypt, Zipporah his wife fends off the divine attack by circumcising her son and striking "his" feet - presumably Moses's feet - with the foreskin. This little episode is obscure in the text as it now stands (Ex 4.24-26). From the standpoint of the themes of the Torah it must be another instance of the testing of the chosen one. Zipporah protects Moses by her act and by saying, "Surely you are a bridegroom of blood to me!" (v. 25)

Hannah is portrayed as a noble figure in I Sam 1. She says nothing in the narrative until she prays to Yahweh of hosts for a son, a prayer that is simple and direct. By contrast, Eli the priest at Shilo rebukes her in formal speech, but upon hearing her respectful, artless response he blesses her. When she conceives and the son is born, she gives him over to God at Shilo, evidently as a nazirite (1.11). So Hannah is not only the determiner of Samuel's life according to I Sam 1, but she also begins the course of events that will lead to Samuel's role of leader and his part in selecting a ruler.

Briefly put, the arche-mother typically stands between the male chosen one and a world which is ofen foreign and hostile. She enables him to realize his vocation by protecting him from the world (Sarah-Abraham, Sarah-Isaac, Moses's mother-Moses, Zipporah-Moses), by launching him toward his destiny (Rebecca-Jacob, Hannah-Samuel), or by acquiring something powerful for him (Rachel-Jacob). In human experience "world" always assumes the form of specific circumstances, persons, and centers of authority. In the mother's role as mediating agent we see the unfriendly aspects of the world as a range of hostile male authority figures: father, father-in-law, king, and God.

C. The Disappearance of the Mother

It is noteworthy that the arche-mother always drops out of the story after some crucial transition is accomplished for one of the divinely favored heroes, whether her spouse or her son. Sarah dies (23.1-2) after the sequence of the birth of Isaac, expulsion of Hagar and Ishmael, and binding of Isaac. This narrative fact, when considered together with the obvious narrative intention of suggesting an analogy between Isaac's relation to his mother and to his wife, could be viewed as a kind of initiatory sequence.[12] The mother bears the son, protects and defends him, he is offered as a sacrifice to

God by his father (but spared), and then the mother dies. In other words, the blessed offspring undergoes a kind of initiation which involves becoming detached from his mother in order to realize his destiny. Elements of an initiation pattern are probably present in many biblical tales. Or perhaps more accurately, the human mind structures experiences around certain common elements and sequences whether in ritual, literature, or social roles.

At any rate, the initiation sequence just stated does not hold in the story of Rebecca. In hatching the plot to further Jacob's progress towards fulfilling the oracle's promise, she incites him to an act that could antagonize the father, and that certainly leads to the hasty departure from both mother and father. But again, after the son flees, or is sent away at Rebecca's behest according to one episode (27.46-28.9), Rebecca disappears from the story as an actor. Thereafter she is mentioned twice in the Jacob narrative (29.12; 35.8) and once in that of Joseph (49.31), but there is nothing about her later life and her death.

After the stealing of the teraphim Rachel is a secondary figure in the story of Jacob until the report of her death. She expires immediately after the birth of her second son, Benjamin (35.16-18).

The egyptian princess does not reappear in the Exodus story after adopting Moses and naming him, and his mother is mentioned only in a later genealogy (Ex 6.20). After the bloody bridegroom episode Zipporah appears only momentarily in Ex 18.2. Hannah has no role after dedicating Samuel to the God of Israel at Shilo. Samson's mother does not appear after Ju 13 except for a brief segment, Ju 14.1-5, in which both parents are seen. The woman of Shunem is met again after the promise scene as she berates the prophet for giving her a son who met an untimely death.

If the underlying theme of an initiation sequence is behind this pattern, it is a theme that would have to be so broadly construed as to be practically vacuous. It may be applicable to the story of Sarah and Isaac (as well as to Hagar and Ishmael), and perhaps to the saving of the infant Moses. It is difficult, however, to discern its features in the other cases. The key to this phenomenon must lie in the intention of the narratives. It has now become a commonplace in biblical studies that the authors and redactors are not interested in "biography" and "autobiography" in any modern sense. They relate what they consider important in light of their understanding of what is at stake in a given story or work. So, for example, what we learn about a prophet's life in the prophetic literature has primarily to do with his prophetic calling. (See von Rad, 1965: 35-36) Assuming this to be a fundamental principle behind what the Bible tells or does not tell, I infer that the arche-mother has a role when she is important in the origins and vocation of Israel. I shall return to this in the final segment of the chapter.

D. Narrative Thinking and the Arche-Mother

The biblical stories of origins are highly sensitive to the anomic elements of history and personal existence, and precisely due to this sensitivity they are concerned with the representation of order[13] - Israel's order as it distinguishes itself from the nations and the mythical patterns of order in the cosmological religions of the ancient near east. The role of the arche-mother is to represent the possibilities and risks of this new order. She is a narrative way of thinking about the pitfalls and potentials of existence in a world where the beauty and fertility of the favored one is threatened by the prospect of barrenness and by foreigners who desire to "take" her, i.e., to assimilate or destroy this new people bearing a new meaning within confusion and chaos (Gen 11.1-9 is the paradigmatic backdrop of this world). Israel is faced continuously with the threat of not-being, of not extending itself into the future; or with the threat of being wrong, disordered, other than she should be. For example, if she "mated" with a foreigner, her children would not be one (= united, under one God).

Her initiative or passivity in the stories of the new order has entirely to do with whether she is being sought by others in this struggle for a new reality or is asserting herself in order to fulfill her proper role as the bearer of a new seed, a new people of history. Understanding her function depends, of course, on how one reads the relevant texts. I view her as always a literary figure, often with great individuality, but also as an expression and interpretation of Israel's meaning in history. That is, she is not "historical," but she represents historicity as a primary image of a new vision of reality which is transmitted and expanded in the history of a covenant people. The argument that she has a typological or allegorical dimension is based on a presupposition and two kinds of textual evidence. The presupposition is that the smaller stories belong to a larger narrative complex of

Israel's history with God which was existentially moving and symbolically meaningful to authors, redactors, and audiences. Thus the ancestors especially, as well as early leaders like Moses, Joshua, and Samuel, are both individual characters and "larger than life"; they are mirrors of Israel's identity. As von Rad has said, "In Abraham and Jacob, Israel saw, increasingly, simply the need and promise of its own existence before God" (1972a: 35). One kind of textual evidence is "internal," i.e., internal to our primary biblical sources for this study, above all the book of Genesis. The use of repetition, as seen in the typic scene, is a key to the presence of supra-individual figures, however much variety and realism may permeate the stories. Such repetition is always a function of convention, which emanates from and addresses itself to communal patterns of meaning. The other kind of textual evidence comes from prophetic voices of the exilic and postexilic periods that depicted Israel in ways reminiscent of the mother stories of the Torah and Former Prophets. The babylonian Isaiah refers to Sarah as Israel's birth-giver (Isa 51.2) and to mother Jerusalem bereft of her children (51.17-23). She is the barren one who will finally be blessed with more offspring than the powerful mistress (Babylon? - 54.1), for her husband (ba^{c}al) is her maker (54.5). In an eschatological poem a prophetic voice envisions Jerusalem giving birth miraculously to sons who will suckle at her breasts (Isa 66.7-11). Such images certainly suggest how the figure of the arche-mother would have been read after the exile (see also IV Ezra 9.38-10.57). In all likelihood the theme of "Israel as mother" is one dimension of the intentionality of the arche-mother stories.

Now when the arche-mother is being sought she is passive and silent. The story-tellers speak of her in these situations as maiden and woman (wife). Some of the same things happen to her time and time again: the male protagonist woos and wins her (for Isaac a surrogate), and she is eventually taken to his land and people. But this new family finds it necessary to move periodically for the sake of its survival, and in these experiences her beauty endangers her male counterpart, for whose sake she allows herself to be possessed (or almost possessed) by the ruler of a given region. She is always extricated from these dangers, much to the benefit of her man, the ancestor, and the manner of relating her liberation indicates that the God will not allow her to be held by foreigners. In the stories of being sought and taken she has little or nothing to say. She has no significant part in the world of dialogue, which is the human world. Thus in these stories she is at the receiving end of words as well as events.

Nonetheless, the narrators tell us, normally very inobtrusively, that she is guided and favored by the God in spite of foreign power and the patriarch's lack of courage. Holding her contrary to Yahweh's designs (which the omniscient narrator knows) will bring disaster to her captors. The God will reveal his will in calamitous events (Gen 12.17) and dreams (Gen 20.3-7) in order to restore her to her rightful place. Presumably even apart from divine intervention the course of events will "conspire" to save her (Gen 26.8-10), although readers will surmise what the narrator evidently wants them to understand: even supposedly fortuitous events are providential for the future of Israel.

The story-tellers also intend to convey that though some things constantly recur, there is nonetheless great diversity within this broad pattern. For instance, the ancestress may be coerced into actual adultery (so presumably in Gen 12), but she is freed in the end and benefits the patriarch. Moreover, she is initially barren, so her issue's future is not affected. This problem posed against the promises is resolved in the divine granting of fertility - the God can cause to conceive where sterility prevails for humans. So much the more Israel knows that its origin is first and finally transcendent. But then when the arche-mother is endangered again, so that the father of her progeny could be in question, her God again steps in (Gen 20). Through a network of speeches in which God even reveals himself to a foreign king, we learn that the king has not touched her, that Abraham is a prophet whose prayers of intercession can restore fertility, and that indeed Sarah is Abraham's sister as well as his wife. Thus the narrative tells us that the ancestors are "royal," a great irony as they are beset by the powers-that-be of the world.

When she asserts herself to fulfill her proper role as the bearer of a new seed, an issue of life which is the embodiment of the new element of promise for the world (Gen 12.1-3), the arche-mother's place in the ongoing story becomes an active one; indeed, she could be described as aggressive. Her proper name is repeated frequently, she has significant speeches, she has the authority to expel the foreign seed and to name her children. The main thing is that when she finds herself unable to conceive she takes decisive steps to remedy the situation. The rival wife, the "other woman," vexes her sorely, belittling her. Nonetheless, she overcomes this other woman, and so comes through the agon successfully. Her success is realized in various ways. Finally, of course, she conceives when the God "smiles" on her. Meanwhile, in the contest stage of her experiences she either has the rival expelled by the patriarch (Sarah) or finally gives birth to the most significant son (Rachel and Hannah).

The "other woman," however, does not disappear from Israel's story. The narratives point to the understanding that every human reality has its other side, sometimes an under side, which will not simply go away. Sarah triumphs over Hagar the Egyptian, a living reminder of the sojourn in Egypt. Still, Hagar's son Ishmael also becomes the father of multitudes. He is associated with "wildness" and peoples of the wilderness; as such he is an agent of defiance and disorder.

He shall be a wild ass of a man.[14]
His hand held against all,
all hands held against him -
opposed to all his brothers shall he dwell. [Gen 16.12]

He reappears in the Joseph story in that his descendants take Jacob's favored son, the dream master born to Rachel, as a slave into Egypt (Gen 37.27-28; 39.1). The descendants of the egyptian slave enslave the favored son of Jacob! Joseph in turn marries the daughter of an egyptian priest and sires two sons by her, Ephraim and Manasseh. Egypt the hated foreign power is, through Joseph, at least partly assimilated into Israel.

Rachel's rival, her sister Leah, was not loved by Jacob. Yet six of the ancestors of the tribes are her sons by birth, and two others are the children of Zilpah her maidservant. Although the story-tellers tell Israel that it is one because Israel stems from Sarah and Rebecca, nonetheless only Joseph and Benjamin are the issue of Rachel, Jacob's favorite and clearly the feminine counterpart to Jacob as Yahweh's chosen one. Even though Leah is unloved by her husband and her eyes are "weak" (Gen 29.17), she and her progeny also have their rightful share in the tradition.

There is an underlying generative principle at work in these origin stories which is simultaneously simple and profound. At the surface, sequential level of the narrative where the different dramatis personae pass through time and encounter one another, the unfavored older "other" is always vanquished or superseded. This holds true whether we are considering Sarah and Hagar, Rachel and Leah, Jacob and Esau, or Israel and Egypt. The lone exception is the story of Cain and Abel, but this fratricide in which the favored shepherd brother is murdered by the older, unfavored farmer brother simply informs us that mankind's origins are out of kelter.

However, in the deeper dimension of the stories where structures and underlying patterns are unveiled, we see that the defeated other is never completely eliminated from the life and reality of the blessed winner. A relationship, some-times close (e.g., Jacob-Esau, Rachel-Leah), remains. To some extent one can speak of the integration of the rival into the chosen one. This assimilation of the rival may not occur immediately. The growth of the seed to be blessed in and by the peoples may take time. So Hagar's role in the larger story is realized only much later in the place of the Ishmaelites as part of the providence working through Joseph's fate. The God of Israel also "has heard the affliction" of Hagar (thus the name Ishmael, "God hears," Gen 16.11) and "has seen the affliction" of Leah (thus the name Reuben, "see, a son!", Gen 31.32). And Joseph marries an egyptian woman! (Gen 41.45) The rival, antagonistic or opposing reality is also part of Israel's make-up. (See Nohrnberg on the "Egyptian/Hebrew dialectic": 37-39.) Moses is recognized as an Egyptian, if not by birth certainly by education. The israelite origin stories intend, of course, to represent this other, this counter-order which poses the possibility of disorder, as dominated and contained in the new order within history that emerges with Abraham and Sarah.

The relation of the God Yahweh to the arche-mother is generally less intimate than to the patriarch. He finally grants her a son or sons, and he hears her prayers. He may even speak to her on occasion (Gen 18.15; 25.23). However, Yahweh is often in communication with the patriarch, prom-ising him a great future and posterity. But Yahweh also tests him. There is therefore considerable ambiguity in the Yah-weh-patriarch relationship. Abraham is required to believe or confirm Yahweh's word of promise, and to believe in God even when the promise seems to be cancelled (Gen 22). As the stories present Isaac he is not asked to believe, but he is laid on the altar by his father as a lad and he is deceived by his wife and younger son as an old man. Jacob prays for the guidance of his God and swears he will worship him if the God will return him safely to Canaan (28.10-22). As he returns at long last to Canaan, he is attacked by an adversary from whom he wins a blessing and a new name and whom he interprets as God himself (32.23-33). Joseph, the great dreamer destined to save not only Egypt but Israel from famine, is thrown into a pit, taken down into Egypt, and cast into prison before he emerges to become eminent in Egypts and pre-eminent among the sons of Israel. He tells his brothers in the recognition scene:

> And now don't grieve or be angry with yourselves that you sold me here, for God sent me before you to preserve life .... So now, it was not you yourselves who sent me here but God .... [Gen 45.5, 8]

Moses is barely rescued from death as an infant and is attacked by his God as he travels to fulfill his mission.

The arche-mother does not enjoy and suffer the same intimacy with the patriarchal God that her husband does. However, there is also an ambiguity about her relation to God, an ambiguity that is not commented on by the narrators; it therefore recedes into mystery. She stands between the male chosen one and the "world" and she disappears after performing a crucial function, whether this be child bearing, protecting the endangered hero, enabling him to prosper, or launching him toward his destiny. After the birth of Isaac and the expulsion of Hagar and Ishmael, Sarah has a part in narrative events only in the report of her death. Rebecca quietly disappears after having guided Jacob to gain his blessing and sent him to her brother in Paddan-aram. Rachel lasts until the Jacob clan returns to Canaan, but she dies while in labor with Benjamin.

So, the arche-mother participates in the faith of Israel, but the fundamental promises are confided to the patriarch. She is the vessel of the patriarch's seed and the God's power to cause conception. The source of continuity is her appearance and disappearance. The primary feminine role in narrative thinking as embodied in the arche-mother seems to be that of continuity and nurture. She is a symbol of ongoing stability; she initiates or enables the heroic journey under God.

However, different roles for the feminine in narrative thinking may be detected in other stories of women, especially the tales of Eve, Deborah, Ruth, and Judith. These stories reflect varying degrees of a counter view, of a sense of anti-order that the feminine personage represents. She is not completely the representation of a dimension of the patriarchally dominated chosen people, but modifies or questions the paradigm of the arche-mother. The woman as counter-order may be viewed very positively or very negatively. She is often quite ambiguous. To these other women we now turn.

Chapter III

OTHER FEMININE FIGURES:
THE MULTIFACETED ISRAELITE FEMININE

NOW WE turn now to these other biblical women whose narrative portraits vary in different ways and degrees from the arche-mother. I have selected these women on the basis of two criteria: they are central figures in a story and they are represented as important agents in enabling the people of God to survive and realize their destiny in the world. The one exception in this discussion is the temptress, who contradicts the order of God through her inauthentic language as she seeks to lure the male figure from right order.

A. Eve: "The Mother of All Living"

Like the matriarchs, Eve is menaced by the "foreign" power, which is embodied in the serpent. It is the latter's sly insinuations that turn God's providential concern into well nigh unbearable restriction. Yet though a divided consciousness emerges as a result of eating the fruit and a deadly penalty is imposed, she and the man have gained something, knowledge of good and evil, which they did not have before. Even though they are expelled from their paradise of succor and harmony, they leave with knowledge "kē?lōhîm," "godly knowledge." In the drama of God and humanity the entrapment of the woman in Gen 3 is the foreshadowing of a recurring pattern of Israel's primary experience in history. The foreign power seeks to take her into his own sphere, and even though she escapes with her life and her man, the enmity of the foreign power continues to weave its way through her experiences.

That the serpent approaches the woman (Gen 3.1-7) - apart from any mythico-psychological interpretation of phallic symbolism, which would push us into the realm of mythical archeology - may be seen as a sign that she is, indeed, that aspect of man, of the duality-in-unity, which is active, aggressive, intelligent. (See Trible: 108-10.) That she is also naive is to say that she has had no experience of craftiness

67

like the serpent's. He entraps her with an opening question which lures her into talking about the prohibited tree. She states concerning the tree in the middle of the garden,

> God said, "You shall not eat from it, nor shall you touch it, lest you die." [3.3b]

It has been conjectured that the woman's addition of the phrase, "nor shall you touch it," which is not in the original prohibition (2.17), shows her anxiety: she is already arguing with herself and trying to convince herself that she is not to do what she wants to do. This conjecture may be correct, but it has a positive side in the woman's make-up. Her anxiety is a function of her intelligence, which seeks to keep her and her mate from danger. Moreover, the literary fact that she does not repeat Yahweh Elohim's injunction verbatim is a sign of the ability to refract and expand what has been communicated. She converts God's statement of permission, "From all the trees of the garden you may certainly eat" (ʔākōl tōʔkēl), into a less authoritarian first person expression, "Of the fruit of the trees of the garden we may eat." In doing so she begins to focus on the fruit, which neither God nor the serpent had mentioned. She also changes all the singular forms of the prohibition to plurals, as though she was "there" when it was given, even if she was not yet formed. Finally she reaches her own conclusion about the fruit of the tree of knowledge of good and evil. Her judgment is not that of a fool or simpleton; within the framework marked out by the serpent's question it has a sound basis, namely, the tree bears food to eat, it is appealing in appearance, and the fruit will lead to godly wisdom. All of this is true in its own context. The other side of it, the "deadly" and alienating aspect of godly knowledge, she could not yet know.

The second thing to emphasize is that the woman is not a temptress or enchantress. It is the serpent that poses the questions and seduces her. Evidently assuming that everything is all right, she eats of the fruit and gives some to the man, who partakes without protest.

This woman of the beginning is, of course, obviously different from the israelite arche-mother. Although the latter is a blood relative of the patriarch in Genesis, the original woman is constructed out of the very body of the original man. This original unity does not become a dichotomy until the emergence of self consciousness and shame after the eating of the fateful fruit. Until then, the story tells us, the pair is a kind of duality-in-unity, perfectly in harmony with each other (2.23-25). The major difference, then, between the woman in the garden and the arche-mother resides in the attempt narratively to conceive and depict a coincidence of opposites which become split off and estranged with the primordial transgression. On the other hand the arche-mother belongs to the representation of a people whose existence presupposes sin and alienation, but who are being divinely led to a new "paradise" (the promised land) and a new community of God and humankind.

We see the narrative thinking about the coincidence of opposites also in the penalties laid upon the three characters in the tale of transgression. The man (ʔādām) is punished by the divine curse on the ground (ʔᵃdāmâ) from which he was taken and to which he will return (3.17-19). He must labor by the sweat of his brow, and his end will be a "dusty death":

for dust you are
and to dust you will return.

The woman is afflicted in relation to the man from whom she was taken. "She shall be called ʔiššâ" (a woman), the man had said, "because from ʔîš (a man) she was taken" (2.23). We know that this etymology is not linguistically accurate in hebrew, but from the narrator's standpoint it prepares the way to depict the female's burdens and possibilities once she knows good and evil. Just as Adam is alienated from his mother matter, the ʔᵃdāmâ, so the ʔiššâ is estranged from hers, the ʔîš. In pain she shall bear children, and she shall be ruled by her man (3.16). As the man must submit to the soil, the woman must yield to the man.

Since the man and woman are penalized with respect to their life sources, it is a fair surmise that the narrator intends to recount something similar of the serpent. He is cursed among all the animals and becomes a belly-crawler and a dust-eater (3.14). Presumably his formerly upright position was related to his cunning (3.1). At any rate, he was formed from the soil like all the animals (2.19), so he is "brought as low" as possible in being called an eater of his own substance. His offspring will be enemies of the woman's offspring. The latter will be a head-bruiser to him, he will be a heal-bruiser to them (3.15).

With the primordial fault and its consequences the archetypal condition of humankind is represented in such a manner as to intimate the situation of Israel in the world. Yet humankind's situation in Gen 2-3 is also different from Israel's because the archetypal picture brings opposites together:

- The man is not at home on the ground from which he is formed. He is alienated from it, and later in the story of Cain we see that he is a wanderer "in it" (bā?āreṣ, Gen 4.12). Yet, as Adam, he simultaneously bears it in himself and will return to it in death.

- The woman is the man's possibility and burden, and she in turn is burdened with pain in bearing mankind. As Adam bears with the ?aḏāmâ, so the ?iššâ bears the ?îs.

When the man names the woman, we encounter an aspect of the story that may be the most puzzling of all. He names her Eve (ḥavvâ), "because she was the mother of all living" (3.20). What is the narrator thinking of here - recalling, reminding, representing regarding the human condition? If "all living" (kol ḥāy) refers to all humans, is Adam excluding himself? Or does he mean that in some basic sense he, too, comes from the woman? But the adjective "ḥāy" is frequently used for any being that we would call an "animal" or that has "flesh," including reptiles (Gen 1.20-21; 2.19; 3.1). Is Eve the mother of all animals? But how could she be? Again, coincidentia oppositorum. Eve is simultaneously Adam or "mankind" ("bone of my bone and flesh of my flesh"), the first woman, and the woman who is named. The narrative itself shows a movement to greater and greater differentiation: species - gender - individual. But with the meaning of the individual name we are turned back once more to her role in the origins of all things: she is "the mother of all living."

Obviously at the surface level of the narrative she is not the mother of all animals. Yet the naming of the woman may imply a riddle, which is the only way to get at the compact denseness of the story's characters, conflicts, and outcomes. The riddle would be, "Why is Eve the mother of all living?" The answer: "Because all other living creatures were created in the search for her, a mate and helper" (2.18-19). If the riddle is restricted to Eve as the mother of all human beings, the answer once again would be rooted in the coincidence of opposites. Eve both receives the "seed" (semen) of Adam and brings forth the "seed" (offspring) of Adam. Since "?āḏām" means here both "humankind" and a man in the story, she is both the mate and mother of Adam.

Eve, as the arche-mother of humankind, is thus obviously different from Israel's arche-mother in that she is the coincidence of opposites, while she is similar in that she is subject to the approach of alien power and is the mediatrix between the man and the "world." But her role as the mate and mother of Adam may offer a clue to the meaning of the family relationships of the matriarchs and patriarchs, which become progressively more distant but still remain close in terms of blood ties: half-siblings (Gen 20) - parallel cousins - cross cousins.[1] In society as we know it, laws about incest exist in order to prevent relatives who are too close from becoming sexual partners, whether because of the dangers of in-breeding, the need for economic exchange, or some other consideration. Whatever the reasons, Israel, too, had its laws defining incest (Lev 18.6-18; 20.19.)[2] The point of the close relationship of the ancestors and ancestresses, especially Sarah and Abraham, is probably an <u>approximation</u> of the coincidence of opposites, as close as Israel could come in its stories of origins to the union of opposites after the downfall and fragmentation of humankind in Gen 1-11. The tradition affirms its origin in <u>one</u> flesh, one reality, but due to strictures against incest the ancestors of the tribes must be the children of the forebears Jacob, Rachel and Leah, who are closely related but just the right distance from one another.

B. Deborah, Jael, Judith:
The Aggressive or Warrior Woman

If one means by "aggressive" the quality of taking initiative or the willingness to compete for some object or objective, the arche-mother and other feminine figures are aggressive when certain things are at stake. The arche-mother competes with the rival woman and strives mightily to be "built up" by having a son. Sarah has the pregnant Hagar, and later Hagar and Ishmael, expelled in order to protect Isaac as heir. Rebecca initiates the deceiving of Isaac which allows Jacob to receive the patriarchal blessing. Rachel steals the teraphim from her father Laban as she and Jacob flee by night.

All of these acts in the narratives are instances of aggressiveness. They are, however, confined to the sphere of relations in the family, and specifically the woman's relationship with husband and son. They are expressions of motherly concerns in a motherly mode. That is, the importance of the arche-mother is subordinated to the larger context of the story of Israel in patriarchal mode, in which the masculine personage is the subject of faith and the central figure of destiny.

The picture of the female heroine is different in other stories, sometimes radically different. We have already taken into account the picture of Eve in Gen 2-3. Eve's peculiar features originate in great part from her function as the "mother of all living," an instance of the puzzle of coincidentia oppositorum. In the story of Ruth and Naomi we shall see tremendous initiative and energy not confined to the theme of the hero's destiny. But here our spotlight is on three women who are aggressive in a sense seldom associated with the human feminine (I am leaving aside the myths of goddesses like Anat and Kali): the readiness to take military measures or to do physical violence in defending one's people. Here the feminine is not simply the embodiment of that new order in history which foreigners would like to grab for themselves and which must therefore be protected. The woman herself is the one who acts to defend and protect her people, while her qualities as female are simultaneously clear in the narrative.

1. Deborah and Jael

Deborah has the most important religious and political role of leadership of any of the women appearing in this study. Judith also has an important part to play as leader, but the social and political aspects thereof are momentary; and in any event, the book of Judith, like Esther, is much more of an allegorized fiction, a kind of ancient jewish "period allegory," than the portrayal of Deborah and Jael.

Is the prominence of Deborah related to the fluidity, indeed the chaos, that the narrator wishes to communicate for the period of the judges? (Polzin: ch. 4) That is, is there some inherent relationship between the instability - the movement between order and anarchy due to Israel's idolatry and deficient leadership - and the importance of feminine personages in Judges?[3] In any case, we see an odd tension between commands or predictions and what actually occurs according to Judges 4. (Polzin: 161-67) The narrator who gives us the larger story (Polzin: the "panchronic narrator") becomes unreliable. Both Yahweh (4.7) and Deborah (4.14) predict that Sisera will be given into Barak's hands, but strictly speaking this does not happen. When Barak finds him he is already a corpse, slain by Jael. The statement that Sisera will be delivered into the power of a woman (4.9)

seems to imply that this would be Deborah, especially given
Barak's affirmation of her charismatic power (4.8), though
the statement is admittedly ambiguous. Since Heber was
allied with Jabin the Canaanite (4.11, 17), Sisera naturally did
not expect to be betrayed by Heber's wife Jael. Yet her
treachery on Israel's behalf is vaunted in Deborah's song
(5.24). What sense can be made of these twists and tensions in
the story and Deborah's song? Let us review chs. 4 and 5 of
Judges before returning to this question.

Deborah is the second of the "judges" in the book of Judges
to whom significant narrative sections are devoted. She is
given three titles: judge (šōpēt), prophetess, and wife of
Lappidot (Ju 4.4). Her power as a prophet is immediately
indicated. She relates Yahweh's command to Barak that he
move in battle against Sisera and the army of Jabin, and
Barak replies that he will obey only on the condition that she
accompany him. She then tells him that his "expedition"
(derek, way) will not be for his own honor, for "into the hand
of a woman will Yahweh give Sisera" (4.9). She subsequently
identifies the day of attack (4.14), evidently part of her
function as prophetess.

In the resulting routing of the troops of Sisera the latter
flees and takes shelter in the tent of Jael, wife of Heber the
kenite. As Sisera sleeps, Jael kills him by hammering a tent
peg through his temple. So Deborah's prophecy is confirmed,
and "God humbled on that day Jabin the king of Canaan
before the Israelites" (4.23).

Jael carries out womanly functions in offering hospitality
to Sisera and attending to his needs. Deborah is identified as
Lappidot's wife, and in the ensuing song is called "a mother in
Israel" (5.7). As "mother" she is simultaneously a woman (i.e.,
wife of a man, perhaps a mother of children) and a leader,
being given precedence over Barak in the prose tale and the
song.

The song in Ju 5 is a stirring battle poem which moves
from martial praise of Yahweh to a description of the
predicament of Israel and of the battle that follows. Jael's
deed is then recounted in a manner that is simultaneously
realistic, exultant, and poignant as Sisera's mother awaits his
return. ("Through her window she looks and peers / mother of
Sisera through the lattice," v. 28.) It ends with an outcry that
hovers between prophecy and wish, approaching a curse:

So may all your enemies perish, O Yahweh,
and his friends be as the sun rising in its strength. [5.31]

Of special interest in this study are the functions assigned to Deborah and Barak: she is to sing, he is to lead the warriors. The symmetry of the poetic parallelism shows that these are both vital charismatic functions.

Awake,awake, Deborah!
Awake, speak (dabbrî) a song!
Arise, Barak, and capture your captors,
    O son of Abinoam! [5.12]

Yet if Barak must arise to guide the troops, Israel is without leadership until Deborah arises as a mother in Israel (5.7).

The poem ends with a juxtaposition of Jael's deed to the mother's impatient wait for the return of her son Sisera. In quantitative terms alone more attention is given to Jael and Sisera's mother than to anything or anyone else in the song (vv. 24-30). The scene of waiting for the warriors' return is effective because the mother's anxiety and the hope for rich booty are so well understood by the poet. It is all the more striking because the waiting scene is preceded by exultation in the bloody deed of Jael that is etched deeply by the technique of repetition that recounts the outcome:

Between her feet he sank, he fell, he lay,
between her feet he sank, he fell,
where he sank, there he lay dead. [5.27]

Three comments about the place of Deborah and Jael in the narrative thinking of Ju 4-5 and the larger context of Judges. First, Deborah's inspired aggressiveness in directing Israel is interpreted by means of the image of "mother." The way of making sense of such a woman is to depict her as like a mother caring for her family. Second and similarly, Jael performs mother-wifely functions for Sisera in entrapping and slaying him.[4] He entered her tent and asked for water; she did even better by giving him milk. As he lay sleeping, having been covered by her with a rug, he thought he was safe, so he slept. So it is that even in their "manly" actions the narrator casts a net of "womanliness" over Deborah and Jael: Deborah succeeds as a "mother," Jael does Sisera in because she knows as a woman how to receive a male guest.

Third, in the context of the narrator's overarching concerns in Judges women have an important place in showing how men do not rule and arrange their affairs by their own might. The book of Judges is complex fictionalized history composed from a masculine or patriarchal point of view that associates men with strength and social dominance but which at the same time appreciates women and the feminine as one of the primary ways that the God of Israel proves that he is the ruler and that all human capablilities and claims will not bring about the desired peace and order in the land. He works also through the (apparently) weak. Deborah asserts to Barak that the undertaking against the Canaanites will not be for Barak's glory, "for Yahweh will deliver Sisera into the hand of a woman" (4.9). Even if the prophecy implies Deborah as the woman, it clearly means in context that the glory will be Yahweh's. Although Jael is "blessed" (5.24), it is Yahweh who leads in battle (5.4-5, 20, 23). The message of the Gideon story is that Israel is not to "vaunt itself" by believing that its human power would save it (7.2). Thus a mere 300 men are chosen to go against the Midianites. However, even though Gideon rejects the title of king, affirming that only Yahweh rules, he becomes ensnared in canaanite religiosity (8.22-28), and his son Abimelech seeks to make himself king in Shechem (ch. 9).

Subsequently Samson, the last of the "judges" whose exploits are recounted, is undone because he betrays the vows involved in his status as a nazirite, and he discloses the secret of his strength to Delilah, the philistine woman (see Crenshaw). After Delilah shaves his hair and he awakes, the narrator's quiet comment is telling: "And he knew not that Yahweh had departed from him" (16.20). The God of Israel works through chosen vessels, the charismatic judges of "deliverers." Unfortunately, however, they are continually tempted to exalt themselves or forget their proper roles, so they do not succeed in establishing Israel's new order in Canaan. One of the divine strategies for showing Israel's weakness and the need to worship Yahweh only, the narrator seems to say, is to use women in bringing the mighty low.[5]

So I have answered the initial question (p.72) in the affirmative: yes, there is an inherent relationship between the story of instability in Judges and the representation of the importance of feminine personages. Women lead or affect the course of history when the times are out of joint. There may be a narrative suggestion in Judges that though women are "weak," they mirror Israel's own situation. Israel, too, is fragile and vulnerable. But Israel is also like women such as Deborah and Jael who are strong when inspired and blessed by Yahweh.

2. Judith

The book of Judith is a diptych whose two panels are perfectly co-ordinated. The first panel, chs. 1-7, relates how Nebuchadnezzar, "the great king, the lord of all the earth" (2.5) sends his army commander Holofernes to conquer all lands to the west because they have disobeyed his word (2.6). Holofernes eventually prepares to attack Bethulia in Judea, in spite of warnings against attacking the divinely guided Israelites. The second panel, chs. 8-16, is a tale of beauty, of militant beauty that overcomes Israel's fear and defeats the dread foreign power. The story is artistically wrought, replete with ironic subtleties and word-plays and with a plot capable of sustaining the interest of the popular reader (see Craven). It is fiction commenting on history, didactic but without such heavy moralizing that one is conscious of reading doctrine rather than a story.

In fashioning this heroine's epic the author employs certain traditional sources in a free manner. He or she must have been familiar with some of the histories such as those represented in Kings and Chronicles. Two crises, the assyrian conquest of Israel in 721 BC and the babyonian exile of the Judeans, are conflated in what may be a deliberate ana-chronism for the sake of the fiction. That the Jews have been in captivity but must once more, even after resettlement in Judah, defend themselves against foreign aggression, may suggest a maccabean or post-maccabean historical setting for the tale.

There are facets of the story that lend themselves to allegorical interpretation, for example, Judith, which means "jewish woman." The possibility of allegorical interpretation is enhanced by the obvious presence of ancient motifs associated with the arche-mother. Judith is a beautiful woman. In 8.7 her beauty is described with the same greek phrase as that used of Rachel and Joseph in the LXX translation of Genesis 29.17 and 39.6 (the hebrew of these two phrases is also the same). Her beauty is so entrancing and ravishing that she is able to entice and undo all the Assyrians who see her (10.4, 6, 14, 19), including above all Holofernes (10.23). Judith's beauty leads to a situation known from the wife-sister typic scene: the foreign ruler desires to take the beautiful israelite woman as his own. Thus Holofernes sends a servant to invite her to a banquet in his tent in order to seduce her at the opportune moment (12.12, 13, 16).

It is likely, too, that the author knows the story of Deborah and Jael. The situation in the tent and the manner of slaying the army commander (13.6-10) are reminiscent of Jael's execution of Sisera. This connection is re-enforced in Judith's song when she exclaims, "but the Lord God Almighty has foiled them by the hand of a woman" (16.6; see Ju 4.9).

But even though the story draws upon ancient sources and motifs, it is an artistic work whose author has freely formed his material and ideas. Judith is a personage who aggressively employs her beauty to deceive the Assyrians and decapitate the assyrian officer. (He loses his head over her!) She is a beauty desired by a powerful foreign male, but she deliberately, with a firm "plan" (8.34), puts herself in the way of the foreigner. She bowls Holofernes over with her loveliness and wise speech (11.21, 23), and the reader knows exactly how cunning she is. For instance, she declares to the Assyrian that "I will not lie to my lord (tǭ kuriǭ mou) this night" (11.5). This is exactly true when seen as double-entente, for she goes on to tell him that "God will accomplish something through you, and my lord will not fail to achieve his purposes" (11.6, RSV). So while Holofernes' purpose to seduce is whirling in his head, God's purpose (= Judith's plan!) of removing Holofernes' head is on the way toward realization.

Moreover, Judith does not follow the dictates of a male dominated society. She calls the elders of Bethulia irresponsible (8.11), she does not accede to Uzziah's request to pray for rain (8.31-34), and she entrusts the management of her wealthy household to a female servant (8.10), whom Judith frees before she dies (16.23). She remains a widow although many men wanted her hand in marriage (16.22). She is apparently childless (16.24), but this in no wise connotes opprobrium in her case.

Judith has an important place in the world of human dialogue, as already indicated. She is one of four biblical women to whom a lengthy song is attributed (Judith 16.2-17; Ju 5; I Sam 2.1-10; Lk 1.46-55). However, hers is unique. Deborah shares her song with Barak, and is the subject in only two verses (Ju 5.7, 12). The prayer of Hannah is a formal psalm that has little directly to do with Hannah's situation. Whatever meaning it has in the beginning of the story of Samuel and the subsequent emergence of the monarchy, Hannah is peripheral to that meaning. Mary speaks only to

77

Elizabeth, and she vaunts God as the mighty deliverer, whereas she herself is the passive recipient of his power: "the mighty one has done great things with me" (or "to me" or "for me" - epoiēsen moi, Lk 1.49). Judith's song is a recital of the events of the tale of Judith (vv. 4-12), enframed by praise of the creator and savior (vv. 1-3, 13-17). Only God is "the great king, lord of all the earth" (see 2.5). A tribute to Judith is the center of the poem (vv. 6-10).

Yet her qualities as a woman are always uppermost in the story-teller's recounting of her deeds. A faithful wife, true to her husband's memory, religiously devout, lovely to look at (8.1-8) - Judith is introduced as though she is the ideal woman on a pedestal. The reader is quickly and somewhat rudely awakened from this assumption as Judith rapidly takes things in hand. Yet as she takes charge she is still the pious worshipper of the one true God, beautiful, faithful, and wise.

Judith is the warrior woman, but always warrior as woman. She embodies one author's narrative mode of thinking about the meaning of Israel's worship of the one sovereign God. Aggressive femininity may be the best approach to life in a world in which there are oppressive foreign powers and false gods. That is, the beautiful Judith serves her people by a piety, beauty and wisdom which she does not maintain passively but puts to active use in defending her people. And in this she is still a "mother," one writer's ideal of the "mother in Israel." Her children are her people, so to say. But as the ideal woman, the "mother in Israel," she is a remarkable portrayal of the other sides of the ideal feminine. She acts in a typically masculine manner when she is aggressive, domineering and belligerent, and she captivates Holofernes and the Assyrians in a fashion reminiscent of the wisdom tradition's warnings against the beauty and wiles of the temptress, the "alien woman" (Prov 6.24-25; Sir 9.8-9; 25.21). Judith as singer and teller of the event is not embarrassed by these wiles; she revels in the "beauty that imprisoned his mind" (16.9).

The specifically jewish theological meaning that emerges from the book of Judith is that whatever the paradoxes involved in Judith's surprising self-assertion and militancy, the defeat of the Assyrians by a woman shows how God can word his sovereign ways through strange vessels that are weak by the world's reckoning (16.6-7). The writer undoubtedly sees an analogy between Judith's virtues as a woman and the situation of Israel as the people of God.

Beauty, piety and wisdom may sometimes have to take the form of seduction, aggressiveness and cunning for God's Israel to be maintained in the world.

C. Esther and Mary:
The Woman as Dependent Heroine

Esther and Mary are two figures very different from each other, but they have two characteristics in common. One is that they are dependent on what others do and so they are rather passive, especially Mary. Mary never initiates any kind of action and Esther does only at the behest of her cousin. They serve ends that finally focus more on masculine roles in the respective stories. This is especially true of Mary, for christian story and art have by and large tended to construe her importance in relation to God the Father and God the Son. Yet even if the two are comparatively dependent and passive, they are nonetheless <u>subjects</u> of stories, which is the second thing they have in common. Unlike the arche-mother who never dominates larger narrative wholes, Esther and Mary are the subjects of story-tellers who depict them in written stories, the book of Esther and the protogospel of James.

1. Esther

In the book of Esther the narrator has everything under complete control. There are no unexpected outcomes, as in Judges; no one out of character, as the pious Judith in her guile; no profound complexities, as in Gen 2-3. Everything is highly stylized.

The Queen Vashti loses her royal standing because she refuses to be shown off as a marvelous beauty to the princes and nobles at the great feast of Ahasuerus. The king's wise men, who "knew the times" (1.13), counsel him to get rid of Vashti lest all the people hear of her ignominious deed and husbands become contemptible in the eyes of their wives. So the Persians maintain order!

In order to replace the queen the king's ministers order that a beauty contest be held, to wit, that beautiful young virgins be brought and prepared to appear before the king. Esther is one of these. She is a lovely young woman raised by her older cousin Mordecai. She wins the contest, gaining the king's favor as the reigning beauty. However, Ahasuerus does not know that she is jewish, for Mordecai has strictly charged her not to disclose this.

Esther is a beautiful virgin, described exactly as are Rachel and Joseph, and as Judith in the Greek: y^{e}pat-tō$^?$ar w^{e}ṯôḇaṯ mar$^?$eh (Est 2.7). She wins a contest involving other women, and she deceives the king "by omission," so to say, as she does not disclose her jewish identity. There are all variations on elements of the typic scene convention of the arche-mother: the beautiful young woman/virgin, the rival woman (here the other contestants), the withholding of the woman's true relationship to the male protagonist. These elements suggest that although Esther is at one level simply the heroine of a historicized fiction, there is a deeper dimension in which she is the "wife" of Israel. This is probably why she and Judith, so unlike in other respects, share certain traits: beauty, faithfulness, childlessness, sexual purity. Being childless is a sign that her true infants are the Israel of the future.

In the events that lead ironically to the rewarding of Mordecai, the hanging of the malicious intriguer Haman, and the royal permisssion for the Jews to slay their enemies, Esther plays an active role only at the instigation, indeed the insistence of Mordecai. He sends her a message

> If you keep completely silent at this time, then relief and deliverance will emerge for the Jews from else-where, but you and your father's family will perish. And who knows whether you have come to royal status for a time like this? [4.14]

In this message Mordecai expresses confidence that the Jews will survive; he appeals to Esther's self-interest, and he suggests that she has a destiny to fulfill. No little pressure.

The message activates Esther, and so here she becomes the active heroine. She commands that the Jews of Susa fast for her, as she and her maidservants will do also, and then she will go before the king without having been summoned - a fearul thing at the persian court as portrayed in Esther. "If I perish, I perish," she says (4.16). Esther goes to the king, is granted an audience, and asks that the king permit her to hold a banquet which the king and Haman would attend. Permission is granted, and thus begins the heart of the satire in which Haman is finally hanged on the gallows that he erected for Mordecai. Poor fellow - though he gets what he deserves, it is an unkind stroke that he is even unjustly accused of trying to rape Esther while the king is in the palace! (7.7-8)

The end of the tale gives much more attention to Mordecai and his new status, although the narrator relates that "the decree of Esther confirmed these matters of Purim; and it was written in the book" (9.32). But the satire closes on the note of the "greatness of Mordecai"; he is the one known for "seeking the good of his people, and speaking peace to all his offspring" (10.2-3).

The book of Esther is a satiric nationalistic fiction with many comic elements. It explains the origin of the festival of Purim and exalts the Jews, while at the same time it affirms life among the gentiles of good will like Ahasuerus. The latter is not very bright, but he is well meaning and at any rate he is the best gentile one has. The tale obviously draws upon ancient babyonian mythic material and revaluates it in order to think of the heritage of the Jews and to think ahead about their possibilities in history. Esther's name is derived from Ishtar. She is Israel's feminine representation who wins the foreign ruler by her beauty. Mordecai is derived from Marduk. He is Israel's masculine representation who triumphs over foreign "wrath" (hāmān)[6] by his knowledge and practical judgment. They are the consort and privy counselor of the king. They guide him perhaps - but they are not the source of authority themselves. They may be viewed as metaphors of Israel in the world, beauty and knowledge which guide and influence but which cannot rule.

2. Mary

Since the New Testament and the christian tradition center in and revolve around one figure, Jesus as messiah, lord and savior, it is naturally different from the jewish tradition for which the locus of divine revelation is the people of the covenant. Thus Israel's salvation history includes many women who participate in and embody the meaning of God's formation of a new human community in the world. Although Christianity has its apostles and saints, its bearer of the divine word is the Christ, so one woman, his mother, has a special symbolic status in christian religiosity.

Here I shall discuss three sources, the canonical gospels of Matthew and Luke and the noncanonical protogospel of James, focusing especially on the latter. In the NT gospels Mary has an important role in the virgin conception and the birth of Jesus (Matt 1.18-25; 2.1-12; Lk 1.26-55; 2.1-20). In both gospels the annunciation follows the pattern of the Old Testament typic scene of the promise to the barren wife.

There are, of course, some variations between the gospels and some elements not found in the Hebrew Scriptures. In Matthew an angel appears to Joseph in a dream in order to reassure him that Mary is pregnant by the holy spirit (1.20-21). Matthew, in keeping with his use of OT quotations and types to structure his story, places the birth at Bethlehem (see Micah 5.1) and fashions it as a kind of recurrence of the egyptian king's attempt to slaughter all hebrew male infants that were born (Ex 1.15-22). Herod thus becomes the "pharaoh" of Matthew's version of the Christ story.

In Luke Joseph plays no part in the annunciation scene, and in the birth account his action is a necessary condition, but only that, for the events that unfold. He takes Mary from Nazareth down to Bethlehem to register there since he is a descendant of David. Luke stresses the virginity of Mary. When the angel Gabriel has made the announcement to her, Mary exclaims, "How can this be? I know not a man!" (1.34) The narrator's introduction of Mary twice describes her as a virgin (1.27). Later on in the genealogy of Jesus Luke adds a parenthetical remark to make the virgin birth clear:

> Jesus ... being the son (as was supposed) of Joseph ....
> [Lk 3.32]

In the annunciation scenes the virginity of Mary is the only radical departure from the ancient jewish typic scenes. The mother is not barren but a young virgin. The young virgin is an image in opposition to the (old) barren woman. (It is worth noting, however, that when the future arche-mother is introduced she is presented as a virgin maiden - so Rebecca, implied of Rachel and the daughters of Reuel; cf. Esther.) But the outcome is the same as in the typic scenes: through a wonderful divine providence the religious hero is conceived in a womb which is not or cannot be brought to conception by the human father. The origin of the son is transcendent, i.e., human deeds and capacities cannot bring it about. For the early christian tradition the virgin birth was a way of saying that the reality of the son Jesus is essentially divine.

This narrative mode of reflecting on the meaning of the new center and bearer of salvation confers special significance on Mary only embryonically in the NT. She plays essentially no part in the story of Jesus after Lk 2.41-42. In Mark 3.31-35 and parallels in Matthew and Luke the importance of Jesus' mother and brothers is minimized in comparison to his "true relatives," those who do God's will. The "mother of Jesus" appears in John 2 and "his mother" stands nearby when he is crucified according to Jn 19.25-27. In both passages she is not named. In keeping with John's christology, she is not really a flesh and blood mother as in Matthew and Luke. John wanted to avoid any connotation of the Christ's birth or existence as a human being (Colwell: ch. III) beyond the bare fact that he came in human form.

Nonetheless, the mother of Jesus begins to emerge in the christian story of salvation by the last quarter of the first century C.E. We have evidence that by some time in the second century, perhaps by 150, she was beginning to assume the religious stature that she would have in subsequent centuries. The proof is the gospel of James (Protoevangelium Jacobi). The gospel of James tells the story of Mary's wonderful birth, her early training, the circumstances of betrothal to Joseph, and the virgin birth of Jesus, ending with the birth of John the Baptist and Herod's murder of the innocents and John's father Zacharias.

In James Mary effects no change except insofar as she is the birthgiver. She animates no one, she intercedes with no one, she deceives no one. She is simply the vessel for the birth of the God-Man. One sign of this is the miniscule part in dialogue that she is given. She first speaks about half way into the story in response to the angel's announcement that she would conceive by the divine word, and her initial words are an interior monologue: "Shall I conceive by the Lord, the living God? As all women do, shall I give birth?" (11.5)[7] After the angel explains that this conception would be by the power of God and that the name of the son would be Jesus, she replies, "Behold the servant-girl of the Lord is before him. Let it be to me according to your word." (11.8; cf. Lk 1.38). Mary speaks three other times, once in response to Joseph's question about her pregnancy (13.9), once to express the vision of two peoples, one in mourning and the other rejoicing (17.8), and then finally to tell Joseph that her time of parturition has come (17.9).

However, if the virgin is an extremely passive figure, two things should still be recognized. One is that she has a story in her own right not completely bound to a human male. In this regard it is interesting that the biblical typic scene of the promise to the barren wife is one of the author's models as he narrates her own conception and birth. Her parents, Joachim and Anna (Hannah), are righteous and wealthy, but

Anna is barren. The Lord's messenger appears first to Anna to promise a child. Anna vows to give the child over as a cultic devotee to God (James 4.1-3), a vow reminding one of the story of Hannah and the parents of Samson. The angel comes also to Joachim to give him the good news, and the happy father-to-be responds joyously by ordering a great sacrifice and celebration (4.4-6). In other words, a type of narrative that hitherto recounted the promise of the hero's birth is now employed to relate the conception and birth of the virgin mother.

The second consideration, closely related to the first one, is that the passivity of the virgin is associated with her complete dependence on God. God is her "mate," so to speak, so human males cannot rule her. She thus hovers between humanity as a female and divinity as an aspect or mani-festation of God.

However, unlike the jewish arche-mother and other femin-ine figures, she is given no hint of another side, of a "counter-order" of any sort. She has no rival whose being is intertwined with hers, and she never acts deceitfully or as a temptress. The "dark side" of the feminine is expressed in the NT with the figure of the whore Babylon in the book of Revelation, and of course there have been the "black cults" of Mary that appear occasionally in the history of Christ-ianity. But by and large she has become a mythical figure which idealizes the passive feminine removed from earthly passions and complexities. This great distance from ordinary humanness and history has intensified the adoration and creativity she often evokes (Greeley), but it also weakens her function as a feminine model for the integration of the complex tensions of existence.

D. Ruth: Woman As Reversal of the Patriarchal Mode

The story of Ruth is in many respects striking and extraordinary. The book of Ruth represents a paradoxical view of the heroine and mother figure. This is signaled by the author's obvious use of the betrothal typic scene. (See Alter: 58-60.) In Ruth we encounter the employment of this convention in reverse fashion, that is, most of the elements of the convention are switched completely to their opposites.

Let us rapidly review the standard features and how they appear in Ruth. (1) The hero travels to a land far away. In Ruth it is the foreign woman, Ruth the moabitess, who travels from her land to Bethlehem of Judah. (2) The hero stops at a well and (3) a maiden comes to the well. These features are not so obvious in Ruth, but are nonetheless present. Boaz tells Ruth to stay with "my maidens" and to drink of the water drawn by the "young men" (n^{ec}ārîm) (2.8-9). Thus Ruth's meeting of her future mate is presumably near a well in Judah and the young men will draw water for her. (4) Hero performs a great feat for the maiden. Boaz, of course, eventually acts on behalf of Ruth by redeeming Elimelech's property and freeing Ruth to be married to him. But prior to that Ruth performs two deeds of extraordinary valor and faithfulness in the eyes of Boaz: she has left her native land and remained faithful beyond the bounds of duty to her mother-in-law (2.11), and she shows him great kindness in not preferring young men to him (3.10). (5) The maiden hurries home to report what has occurred and (6) the stranger is invited into the household of the maiden. Ruth assumes the typical role of the maiden in reporting to Naomi what occurred when she met Boaz, but Boaz is not invited to the dwelling of Naomi and Ruth. Rather she takes, at Naomi's behest, the audacious step of lying beside Boaz as he sleeps during harvest-time on the threshing floor. In other words, she approaches him on his own terrain to set in motion the process leading to redemption of the land and betrothal. The marriage may be viewed as the full integration of Ruth into judean society. (7) Hero marries maiden at the well, and eventually returns with her to his own country. Ruth marries Boaz, whom she meets near a well, and remains in his native land to which she came as a foreigner.

This turning over of the betrothal typic scene so that a woman comes from the east to Judah in Canaan intimates a revolution of literary and religious imagination. Here we find two women as completely active heroines. Ruth receives instructions indeed, but not from a man; it it Naomi who guides and animates her. When Naomi is about to depart from Moab, Ruth clings to her (dāb^{e}qâ-bāh) and pleads, "Entreat me not to abandon you" (l^{ec}āzbēk) (1.14, 16). One can hardly avoid recalling, as other interpreters have done, the conclusion of the creation of woman in Gen 2: "Therefore a man shall leave (y^{ac}azāb) his father and mother and cleave (w^{e}dābaq) to his woman, and they shall be one flesh" (Gen 2.24). (See Trible: 197, n.13.) But Ruth the young widow abandons her home and family out of her love for Naomi, her mother-in-law.

After the death of her husband and sons, Naomi wishes,

quite normally, to return (wattāšob) from Moab to Bethlehem
(1.6, 7). Her two daughters-in-law accompany her part of the
way, and she then commands them to return (lāšûb) to their
mother's houses (1.8), but they reply that they would return
with her to her people (1.10). But Naomi exhorts them:

> "Turn back [šōbnâ], my daughters, why go with me? Have
> I yet sons in my belly to be your husbands? Turn back
> [šōbnâ], my daughters, go on, for I am too old to be a
> man's ...." [1.11-12]

Orpah turns back. Ruth, however, continues to cling to Naomi. The dialogue continues (vv. 15-16):

> "See now, your sister-in-law has returned [šābâ] to her
> people and to her God. Go back [šûbî] after your sister-
> in-law." And Ruth said, "Entreat me not to abandon you,
> to turn back [lāšûb] from following you, for where you
> go, I will go, and where you lodge, I will lodge; your
> people shall be my people and your God my God ...."

So Ruth refuses to return to her own family, but turns to
Naomi as her object of love, and returns with her to Judah.

The radicality of Ruth's act is comparable to the story of
Abraham. But Abraham was called by God to go to a land he
did not know, whereas Ruth obeys her human feelings. For
such a story to be told about a woman who was to become,
according to this tale, the ancestress of David, suggests that
masculine models no longer sufficed as the author sought to
articulate the meaning of the heroic journey, human loyalty,
trust in the God of Israel (whom Ruth worships as a consequence of attachment to Naomi), and Israel herself. Concerning the people Israel, the little story ends with the note
that Ruth's son, Obed, is the grandfather of David.

Ruth, counseled by Naomi, grasps the thread of events in a
fashion that enables the reader to know that divine providence is structuring the story even as human beings act
according to understandable needs and desires. Thus she plays
masterfully on Boaz's blessing upon her in 2.12. Boaz says:

> "May Yahweh reward your deed; may you have full re-
> compense from Yahweh God of Israel, under whose wings
> [kᵉnāpāyw] you have come to be sheltered."

Later Boaz awakes to discover Ruth lying beside him on the
threshing floor. She says,

"Spread your cloak-skirt [keٔnāpekā] over your maid-servant, for you are redeemer." [3.9]

The Hebrew "kānāp," "wing," means also "skirt," or the loose, flowing end of a garment. When Ruth asks Boaz to spread his kānāp over her she is inviting him, in effect, to be the agent of the divine blessing that he had wished for her.

It could be, of course, that this short story addresses itself to the question of exclusivism and specifically the expulsion of foreign wives in the period of the reforms of Ezra and Nehemiah. As already discussed in ch. I, establishing such a historical and social context may provide us with the necessary condition - provenance and problematics - for our reading of the text. Knowledge of this sort, however, is not the sufficient condition for interpretation, and in this case it certainly does not exhaust the beauty and meaning of the story, which avoids all didactic and moralizing tendencies.

Moreover, by not adhering to the letter of the Torah's regulations concerning foreign wives (who belonged to various ethnic groups in Canaan and did not include Moabites) the narrow nationalists were being legalistic to a remarkable degree. As David Clines has shown, their interpretation of the laws, whose objective was to avoid marriages outside of the recognized israelite clans and tribes, was both legalistic and in keeping with the intention of the laws. Thus the exclusivists would hardly have been impressed with a moabite heroine of faith, for they already had to hand the religious and legal basis of their reform and this despite existing stories in the Torah about forefathers who married foreign women (Abram, Joseph, Moses). This said, the possibility that Ruth was written in such a historical context still remains; in fact, dating it to about this time makes good sense. One wonders, however, whether the author could then really have hoped to change attitudes in the prevailing circumstances.

Still, a close reading of Ruth leads to the conclusion that the ancient hebrew writer found patriarchal religion inadequate, or we can say at least, à la Booth, that the "implied author" intends to give us his narrative thinking on the subject. To put it another way, only a foreign woman could embody what he wanted to say - even a Moabite who, according to Deut 23.4, could never enter into Yahweh's assembly. The only qualification of this questioning of patriarchal values is the frame of the book (1.1-2; 4.18-22). The author employs traditional devices in the opening and closing passages. The former focuses on Naomi's husband and sons, shifting to Naomi herself in v. 3 ("Elimelech, husband of Naomi"). The latter is a genealogy from Perez to David. This conventional frame may have secured the story a reading it would not have had otherwise.

In any event, Ruth is represented as the authentic Israelite. The play on "šûb" (turn, return) in ch. 1 may be a way of suggesting that an authentic dimension of Israel "returns" to Judah in the form of Ruth. One aspect of the authentic Israelite is a foreign woman. She goes to an unknown land out of love for her israelite mother-in-law, she takes refuge under the wings of the God of Israel, she shows "hesed" ("kindness" or "steadfast love") to both Naomi and Boaz, and she bears a son whom Naomi nurses in her old age.

E. Delilah, Potiphar's Wife, and the Alien Woman in Proverbs: The Temptress

The temptress in biblical thought is strange, foreign, a "shadowy other" to the ancient israelite thinkers. The three biblical narratives in which a temptress is a primary agent are the tale of Delilah and Samson in Judges 16,[8] of Potiphar's wife and Joseph in Genesis 39, and the alien woman in Prov 7.6-27. In Proverbs the temptress is called a "foreign woman" (zārâ) or an "alien woman" (nokriyyâ). Potiphar's wife is, of course, an egyptian woman, and Delilah lives in Sorek ("vine"), presumably in philistine territory. At any rate, she serves the Philistines in undoing Samson.

Joseph, like his ancestress Sarah, is brought into a situation of moral danger (Rebecca, too, is nearly endangered - Gen 26). His situation is precisely the obverse of the matriarchs: a foreign woman desires him due to his beauty, and the outcome of the sexual affair could have been the execution of Joseph for adultery. This in turn would have meant the end of Israel, for in God's providence Joseph is betrayed by his brothers and sold as a slave into Egypt in order to enable Israel to survive (Gen 45.6-8).

There are two primary features of Potiphar's wife as a temptress: she attempts to seduce Joseph and she lies about what happens. She beseeches him continually, "Lie with me" (Gen 39.7, 10). One day when no one else was in the house,

> she caught him by his garment, saying, "Lie with me."
> And he abandoned his garment in her hand, and fled, and
> ran away. [39.12]

She calls the servants in order to pretend that Joseph tried to

rape her, and when her husband returns she makes the same accusation. In making the charge she cleverly lies by reversing facts and by subtly insuring that the facts will be misconstrued. To the servants she maintains:
- That the Hebrew came in "to me to lie with me." (This is what she had desired.)
- That she cried out "with a loud voice." (This is not reported in the incident, but if she did it would have been first in outrage over rejection and then a false cry of rape.)
- That "he abandoned his garment beside me." (He "abandoned" his garment in her hand when she clutched at him.)
In putting her case before the servants she declares that her husband had brought in a hebrew slave "to mock us." She repeats this allegation against her husband when he comes home: "The hebrew servant, whom you have acquired for us, came to me to mock me." She then repeats what she told the servants. Potiphar is thus faced both with an accusation against Joseph and against himself: it was he who had brought this nasty hebrew seducer into the house!

The interrelation of seduction and lying language is narrated differently in the tale of Samson and Delilah. Here there is no question of sexual seduction, although Delilah uses Samson's commitment to continuing sexual relationship as a means of undermining him. Assuming the power of her sexual attractiveness, she acts for the Philistines in "enticing" or "seducing" him to give up the secret of his invincible strength (Ju 16.5). Whether Delilah is supposed to be a prostitute is not clear. She is called simply "a woman," although the Delilah narrative is immediately preceded by a short account of Samson's visit to a harlot in Gaza (16.1-3). At any rate, Delilah agrees to uncover Samson's secret for an enormous sum of money.

Three times she tries to pry the secret from him and each time he gives her a false answer. It is a highly stylized story that would be ridiculous if one were expecting a rich, experientially oriented account. As it is, Samson is represented as absurdly stupid for continuing to traffic with a woman in whose dwelling Philistines lurk to jump on him after each incorrect answer he gives. Of course, the story-teller never says that Samson is bright.

Finally Delilah has had enough of this:

"How can you say, 'I love, you,' when your heart is not with me? These three times you have mocked me and

> have not told me in what your great strength lies." And
> so it was that when she pressed him daily with her words,
> and urged him, his soul was vexed to death. [16.15-16]

So Samson finally yields and reveals the secret.

Delilah seduces Samson into giving up the secret of his strength by playing on his sexual attachment. This sexual infatuation is the necessary condition of his downfall, but not the sufficient condition. The sufficient reason is her ability to use language in a certain way: she appeals to his love for her and nags him daily.

In Prov 7.6-23 the "alien woman" (zārâ/nokriyyâ) is depicted by the sage-father speaking to his "son" (7.1). He leads up to the little narrative segment by urging the listener-son to call wisdom his sister and understanding his kinswoman in order to protect himself from the smooth words of the temptress (7.4-5). Then the sage assumes the role of voyeur as he describes the empty-headed young man in a nighttime assignation with the seductress. The heart of the narrative is the speech ascribed to the woman (vv. 14-20), which the narrator characterizes as seductive blandishments (v. 21). She tells the fellow that she has discharged her vows of sacrifice (v. 14), implying that her life is in order and that there is nothing out of the way about her proposition. Furthermore, the meat remaining from the sacrifice would be available to eat. So the timing is perfect: vows discharged, meat to eat, a bed perfumed for love-making (v. 17), and her husband away on a long business trip (vv. 19-20). The young fool yields (vv. 21-23) as "an ox led to the slaughter," as "a bird hastens to the snare." The sage-voyeur concludes with a peroration warning against the alien woman (vv. 24-27), for her ways are deadly.

Elsewhere in the book of Proverbs this picture is reinforced in proverbs and extended aphoristic reflections. The portrayals highlight the temptress as a figure of disorder in her seductive abuse of language. The relation of the seductive siren and the misleading mouth is caught in the clever image of Prov 22.14:

> The mouth of strange women is a deep pit:
> One abhorred by Yahweh will fall therein.

The association of seductive language, sex, and death ("deep pit") is unmistakable (cf. Prov 23.27). It is the alien woman's coaxing words (2.16; 6.24), her honeyed words (5.3), which hold the power of entrapment. The temptress, the alien, strange woman, the siren, leads the man astray from self-discipline, proper family life, and generally from right social order. This right order has its center and focus in language.

Interestingly, in Proverbs there are two feminine figures, or realities personified as women, who offer a sharp contrast to the temptress. One is Wisdom, the other Language. The former appears in the form of a woman in Prov 1-9. Dame Wisdom appears in the streets and squares to call humans to her (1.20), she is a "tree of life to those who lay hold of her" (3.18), and she plays and delights in the world of mankind (8.31). There is thus more than a hint of the sexual about her. However, her function is to establish peace and order. She does not want human beings to be wayward and foolish (1.32), her ways are pleasant "and all her paths are peace" (3.17). She is understanding, she is the first principle of God's creation (8.22), she constructs the house of order (9.1ff.). She is in every way the contrary of "the woman Folly." (9.13).

Dame wisdom is a symbol of order, and as such she is the basis and object of right language and right conduct. But there is one noteworthy instance where the common word for language is used in the trope of a feminine personage. The hebrew word is "lāšôn," the common noun for "tongue," but which means also "language." She appears in this proverb:

Death and life are in the hand of the tongue,
and her friends will eat of her fruit. [18.21]

The tongue - "language," with special stress on speaking - is a noun of feminine gender. She has fruit in her "hand" (yād, usually translated "power"), a fruit which brings death or life to her "friends." The word for friend, "ʔōhēb," means also "lover." The image of the lovers of language is reminiscent of the adherents of Dame Wisdom:

I love my lovers,
and my seekers shall find me. [8.17]

That the fruit in 18.21 is held out by "lāšôn" there is no doubt: "death" and "life" are both masculine nouns, so the possessive pronoun attached to "fruit" must refer to the tongue. Here again we come to a suggestion of the sexually alluring in a positive figure of order. The image of a feminine figure offering fatal or vital fruit to her lovers plucks the chord of a paradise myth, that of the woman offering the fruit of knowledge of good and evil to the man. Language is the potential of death and life in a human world, and as such she is inherently more ambiguous than her sister Wisdom. Wisdom cannot be other than the charm of divine order. Language can become distorted and so offers the possibility of deception and death as well as truth and life.

In sum, the temptress in biblical literature is a figure of the strange, alien, shadowy "other" in which one may lose one's bearings, one's sense of order. The disorder that she embodies is expressed not so much in her beauty or sexual wiles as in her manner of using language. In the larger story of Israel she appears in Potiphar's wife as a foreign figure posing the potential dissolution of Israel as represented in Joseph. In Delilah she appears as the seductive seeker of Samson's secret; Delilah is indeed the primary agent of Samson's destruction, thus ending any confidence - so the narrator intimates - that Israel could place in the charismatic judges. In Proverbs the alien, seductive siren is an important figure, not only as an actual type of person who is dangerous to the male but as a metaphor of disorder in her misleading use of language. Two figures contrary to the temptress are Wisdom as a symbol of divinely grounded peace and order, and Language as a metaphor of the possibility of constituting a human world.

Let us observe, however, that the biblical stories do not draw up an absolute, clear-cut line of separation between the temptress and Israel's heroines. In the function of the woman as an agent of transformation we find that the fundamental change of situation that she effects involves, characteristically, the deception of some domineering male, viz.:

- Rebecca, who animates Jacob to deceive Isaac and gain the patriarchal blessing.
- Rachel, who steals her father's teraphim and then conceals them when he has chased Jacob, Rachel and family down. It is possible that the teraphim, probably icons of household gods, represented a claim to Laban's propery (so Speiser: 250), and probably the theft is also intended to increase the power, the numinous undergirding, of the Jacob clan.
- Moses' mother, who conceals him; the egyptian princess, who draws him from the water and presumably conceals his origins from her father the king; and Moses' sister, who manages to put herself in a position to take Moses back to his mother to be nursed for the princess!
- Jael, who gets Sisera into a vulnerable position to slay him by pretending to perform the office of hostess for her guest.

92

In all these stories the feminine is the agent of change for a male person or her people in a world which threatens the tenuous existence of God's new order in human history. But there is one instance, already discussed, in which the favored woman, the one with whom the narrator sides, appears as a "temptress" in the precise sense already delineated: sexual seductiveness centered in lying language. This instance is Judith. She captivates and eventually decapitates Holofernes through her beauty and wise speech (Judith 11.21, 23). Her involvement with Holofernes is played out through a grand double-entente in which the narrator and audience know that Judith's deceptive speech to Holofernes simultaneously alludes to the truth from the perspective of God (11.5-6). Judith becomes a "deep pit" to Holofernes the Assyrian!

There is another biblical story whose heroine may appear at first reading to be a "temptress." This is the tale of Tamar and Judah, Gen 38. (See Alter: 3-12). As is characteristic of biblical narrative, the story is laconic to the point of being elliptical about Tamar's intentions and the details of her appearance as she stations herself in Judah's way (38.14). The ironic turn of events does, however, make it clear that Tamar planned an outcome that would rectify the wrong done to her. Nevertheless, Judah is "seduced" because he wants the woman and views himself as the aggressor. There is no indication in the text that the disguised Tamar tries to allure Judah. He sees her as a prostitute and strikes a deal with her in a dialogue that depicts "business as usual" (38.16-18):

Judah: "Look here, let me have sex with you.
Tamar: "What will you give me to have sex with you?
J.: "I'll send you a kid from my flock.
T.: "If you give a pledge until you send it.
J.: "What pledge shall I leave with you?
T.: "Your seal and cord, and the staff in your hand."

So they have sex and she conceives by him.

Here there is no flattery, cajoling, or lying in the ordinary sense. Tamar lets Judah believe what he wishes to believe. When later he is informed that Tamar is pregnant "by harlotry" (38.24), he brutally commands that she be executed by burning. She then sends him the seal, cord, and staff, asking him to recognize them (38.25); he recognizes them and acknowledges that she is in the right in that he had not allowed the levirate obligation to be fulfilled (38.26).

At a deeper level of the respective accounts, the designs and actions of Judith and Tamar are very similar in the basic conflict that generates the specific drama: both represent the truth or the right as they understand it in their respective situations, and both allow the male antagonist, who serves untruth or injustice, to believe what his mixture of desire and conventional expectations lead him to imagine. Here we touch upon a profound aspect of the temptress trope, namely, her existence as a figure of disorder and dishonest language stems in great part from the propensity of males to deceive themselves and imagine themselves as sexual conquerors. This male propensity is the "matter" that that narrators form and refine in order to show how Samson was undone through obtuseness and infidelity to his calling, and Holfernes lost his head because he thought he could deceive Judith and take her great beauty for himself.

Chapter IV

THE SYMBOLIC FUNCTIONS OF THE FEMININE

IT IS apparent that there are mythical elements in the arche-mother stories. That is, there are acts, situations, and themes known from the cosmological myths of the ancient near east and other areas of the world. There are some interpreters who use the term myth as a word comprehending all stories in which the divine, otherworldly, or ideal is related in terms of the human, this-worldly, or real.[1] Those biblical passages are taken as mythic which disclose not only parallels to cosmological myth, but also show allusions or archaic survivals in metaphorical expressions.

While this use of the word has its justification, and is certainly well-nigh ubiquitous among religion scholars, the word "myth" is considered inappropriate for the purposes of this study. Myth is stylized in form and represents characteristically an enclosed world view. Hebrew narrative, on the other hand, is a highly flexible, adaptive technique which shows a world in process of being created.

If one compares the story of creation in Gen 2 and the subsequent interplay among Adam, Eve, the serpent and Yahweh with any ancient nonbiblical story of the origins of humankind, one will fail to find elsewhere the richness of narrative tension and irony, the indications of interior consciousness through action and speech, and the movement toward a history yet to be resolved. Or if one were to compare the biblical references to God's slaying of a dragon to ancient near eastern texts, one finds not only that the biblical occurrences are brief, sometimes passing references, but more importantly they are placed within the context of the ongoing story of God and Israel. So in Psalm 74.12-14 the recounting of the battle with Leviathan is located in the middle of the hymn; it is the occasion of affirming faith in the creator God who can save his people and should remember the covenant (v. 20), for he has rejected his people and the temple is in ruins. Likewise the prophet's affirmation in Isa 51.9-10, which is in the form of a mythical reference:

> Aren't you the one that hews Rahab,
>> that pierces Tannin?
> Aren't you the one that dries up the sea,
>> the waters of the great Tehom?
> That makes the depths of the sea
> the way for the redeemed to pass over?

I have translated the verbs in the present tense here because the hebrew forms are participles, giving a sense of present rather than past acts. The context is the prophet's call for the "arm of Yahweh" to redeem his people in exile. It is followed by the divine response, "I, I am he, your comforter" (51.12). The literary form is that of a divine-human dialogue between the prophet (representing Israel) and Yahweh. The concern is redemption within present historical existence. The difference in degree is so great betweeen this form of religious and literary expression and that of the ancient near eastern cosmogonies, theogonies, and other tales of deities and heroes that it amounts to a difference in kind.

Thus I shall speak of the symbolic functions of the arche-mother, although I recognize the relation of these functions to elements of cosmological myth. The functions pertain to origins, love and inspiration, and change of life-situation (decisive transition). After the review of these symbolic functions of the arche-mother, there will be a consideration of the feminine personages whose qualities and acts modify, question or deny the composite picture of the arche-mother. Assuming that the arche-mother represents a dimension of Israel as a divinely given order in the world, I intend to survey those figures who represent two kinds of counter-order: a positive counter-order which the narrator approves and which moves within God's design for Israel, and a negative counter-order that the given implied author disapproves as alien, as anarchic vis-à-vis the true order of things for Israel or, as in Proverbs, for proper human adaptation to the world order.

A. Origins, Love and Inspiration, Change

It is obvious that the arche-mother is typically the mother of a significant son, the progenitress of descendants who are Israel. That Israel knew of its origin in varied and fragmented peoples (so Gen 10 and 11), and that not all the tribes were sprung from the same wife of Jacob, made it even more important to affirm the beginnings in Sarah. It is thus even more striking that the stories relate not only a threat to Sarah's status as wife of Abraham which one might expect, but a danger stemming from the patriarch himself! The ancestor's desire for survival - with a little wealth thrown in! - endangers the arche-mother.

The theme of the endangerment of Israel's progenitress by the patriarch is a complexity composed of elements of Israel's historicity and the symbolic functions of the arche-mother. The element of historicity resides in the knowledge that in order to survive, Israel tends to sacrifice something essential to its identity. Yet without survival, there is no identity to maintain. The arche-mother is so desirably beautiful that foreigners prize her, and through allowing foreigners to have access to her the patriarch can prosper. It is as though she is the patriarch's source of nurture in an alien environment.

The mother's role as progenitress and source of nurture is intimately related to her function as an agent of change who enables the chosen one to overcome obstacles as he moves towards the fulfillment of God's promises. We have already discussed the acts of the arche-mother which protect or otherwise aid the male recipient or transmitter of the promises (ch. II, B.). She is portrayed variously as protecting him from the world, launching him toward his destiny, and acquiring a boon for him. In standing between him and the "world," she may transfer something from the world or enable the goods of the world to come to him, she may give him his chance to move successfully into the world, or she may actually determine his destiny (Rebecca-Jacob, Hannah-Samuel).

The ways in which this mediating function are accomplished are so varied that they are another sign of the author's use of a common symbolic theme with great flexibility and artistry. Often the narrative result is a representation of contrasts in the same character that heighten their credibility, and thus the reader's sense of an actual world, while at the same time one knows that Israel as a symbol[2] is always present in the current of events. How passive Sarah can be in the wife-sister scenes, but what a "bear" when it comes to protecting Isaac! The integrity of Rebecca ranges from her acquiescent politeness to her shrewdness as a strategist in getting the blessing for Jacob. Hannah is modest, inherently noble, and willing to offer to God the very

gift of a son that God had granted her. Rachel is beautiful
and bitchy, and does not hesitate to lay hold of numinous
objects for Jacob.

Now the ubiquity of the guiding or mediating feminine
personage is well known in various cultures and in all sorts of
human wisdom. They include a wide range of figures, e.g., the
harlot associated with Ishtar and the city of Uruk who
"civilizes" the wild man Enkidu in the Gilgamesh epic, the
regenerating powers of the goddess Anat whose dessication of
Death revives Baal in the ugaritic myth, and the Dame
Wisdom who is a kind of psychopomp of life (Prov 3.17-18)
and immortality (Wisdom 6.18; 8.13). One is reminded also of
Paghat's quest to avenge the murder of her brother Aqhat in
the canaanite tale. She dresses as a warrior with female garb
as outer clothing, and finds his murderer. At this point the
story is thematically similar to Judith's deed. The text breaks
off, but cuneiform scholars conjecture that Paghat killed
Yatpan while he was asleep intoxicated, and that somehow
Aqhat was restored to life (H. Ginsberg in Pritchard: 155;
Coogan: 30). We meet the mediating feminine again in the
arche-mother, but with three distinctively israelite differences: (1) she is completely human.[3] (2) She appears always as an individual character, with human virtues and
foibles, even as she represents this universal theme of the
mediatrix. (3) As a psychopomp, or more precisely an
"ethnopomp," she acts for the sake of her child Israel in the
story of God and Israel.

As a beauty desired by foreigners, as progenitress of the
promised people, and as agent of change it is small wonder
that she is an object of love and inspiration. Though the
number of passages are few and often brief that express a
feeling of wonder about her, they are nonethless telling. Why
would the Egyptians and the people of Gerar pay so much
attention to the wife of the patriarch? Even if she was
beautiful, why would the kings single her out? We have to
reckon of course with the simple need of the story to recount
the predicament in which Israel's ancestors often found
themselves, but the narrative fact remains, she is very
special. For Isaac, as we have observed, it is as though the
mother's absence is not filled until Rebecca becomes his
wife. The one-word predicate in Hebrew, "wayye?eḥābehā,"
"and he loved her" (Rebecca, Gen 24.67), is simultaneously a
statement of his love for Rebecca and a poignant comment
on his feeling for his mother.

Concerning Rebecca, her attractive qualities are so great that they become a witness to divine providence as the old servant of Abraham searches for an aramean wife for Isaac. She is a terrific find. The servant had imposed rather demanding conditions on God in praying for success (Gen 24.12-14). The silently working "angel" (v. 7) brings about an immediate fulfillment of the prayer, and the damsel turns out to be a dream. Not only does she do what the servant requested in his prayer, but she is "very good looking, a virgin, and no man had touched her" (v. 16). Whether or not the servant knows of her virginity, which the omniscient narrator emphasizes, he sees enough to know that everything is coming to pass beyond his fondest expectations. He is thus thrown off-guard in what the narrator probably intends as a humorous comment (v. 21; see Landy: 15-16).

And the man was gazing at her speechless, to know whether Yahweh had made his journey successful or not.

When Jacob first sees Rachel, he becomes excited and strong enough to roll away the stone from the well by himself. The scene is full of humor:

And it happened that when Jacob saw Rachel daughter of Laban his mother's brother, and the sheep of Laban his mother's brother, he up and rolled the stone from the mouth of the well. [Gen 29.11]

The sheep are also of no little importance to Jacob! But that the arche-mother is associated with prosperity or potential prosperity simply reinforces the point concerning her desirability. It is significant that Jacob offers to enter into servitude seven years for Rachel after her beauty is noted in the narrative (29.17).

And Jacob loved Rachel. And he said, "I will serve you seven years for Rachel your daughter." [29.18]

In performing these symbolic functions the arche-mother is not an initiator of action outside of the family circle. Though Sarah does "kindness" (Gen 20.13) for Abraham in Egypt and Gerar, hers is a passive role with no part in the extra-familial world of conversations and action. Rebecca sends Jacob out into the world, so to say, but she does not deal directly with anyone outside of the family. Nor does Moses's mother.[4] One possible exception to this pattern is Hannah, who speaks twice to Eli the priest of Shilo and dedicates Samuel as a

99

nazirite there. However, both speeches are humbly polite, and the first one is a response after Eli speaks to her. Her first words are a vow to Yahweh in which she shows herself to be so desperate for a son that she promises to give up the very son who would fulfill her hopes. Most of the women now to be considered, however, have active roles ouside of the bounds of the family.

B. The Woman As Counter-Order

1. Positive Counter-Order

The first two feminine figures to be considered are linked by the fact that they are not loved by the patriarch. They are not objects of love and inspiration, although they are signifiant as progenitresses.

Leah is especially interesting because she is clearly not the one favored by Jacob. The narrator wants us to know that Rachel is the counterpart of Jacob, a sort of "Jacobah" (Fokkelman: 163). She is beautiful, but barren. She, like Jacob, is able to deceive and to hold on to what she has. She steals Laban's household gods and she adumbrates Jacob's encounter with the Adversary at the Jabbok when she names Bilhah's second boy Naphtali, saying, "With godlike struggles (naptûlê ʔeॡlōhîm) have I struggled with my sister, and I have prevailed" (naptālî, Gen 30.8). She wins out over her sister in the sense that she is the primary matriarch and the mother of Joseph, who dominates the latter part of Genesis.

Given the apparently inferior status of Leah, it is a fascinating narrative fact that she is the birth-mother of six of the sons of Jacob, and two others are by her servant Zilpah. Thus the storytellers of Israel recognize that two-thirds of the eponyms do not come from the favored matrilineal side, and only two of them were borne by Rachel. Leah avows, of course, that though Jacob does not cherish her, God cares for her nonetheless (29.32-33). The tenuousness of the relationship of the tribes is thus built right into the heart of Israel's story. The problem is solved at the divine level, so the narrator discloses, even though at the level of human relations there is an inherent tension in the larger family. Though the patriarch does not love one of his wives, God does; so it is that a superordination is effected - the divine blessing encompasses that part of Israel which Israel (Jacob) did not really want.

Now Jacob and Esau are twins, so closely related that they

are born almost simultaneously. Already at birth Jacob is not to be left behind (25.26)! This twofold unity has to be divided in the ensuing drama, but not without indications that Jacob's grasp on numinous power and blessing is bound up with his relation to his brother. He dreads the encounter with Esau as he approaches Canaan. He then meets up with the Adversary who he concludes is God, so he names the site of the struggle Face of God (32.31). When he is reunited with Esau he tells him that seeing his face is like seeing the face of God (33.10). As Esau is the human alter, in some sense the shadow side of Jacob, so Leah is Rachel's alter - but integrated into the line of the divine promise. On the paternal side the "other" is eliminated from Israel at the diachronic level of the drama, on the maternal side it is incorporated. This maternal other, Leah, bears the only daughter mentioned (Dinah, Gen 30.21). It is this daughter and two of Leah's sons, Simeon and Levi, who are to be the occasion of embarrassment for Jacob in Canaan (Gen 34). Through the unloved one there is strife within the Jacob clan.

Tamar is the ancestress of David as the mother of Perez (Gen 38.29). Her decisive actions in Gen 38 call attention to her determination and Judah's inconstancy. She is unloved, but she protects her rights and so becomes a memorable figure in the genealogy of Israel. Gen 38 begins with the report that Judah "went down" (wayyēred) from his brothers, an odd statement here, but perhaps it is to be related to the beginning of ch. 39: "And Joseph was brought down (hûrad) to Egypt." Although the Judah-Tamar episode seems to be an interlude in the flow of the Joseph story, the use of the root "yrd," "go down," is one of the many signals that the narrator has it constantly in mind (Alter: 6).[5] Judah takes a canaanite woman, whereas Joseph resists the advances of an egyptian woman. Judah promises to send Tamar a young goat. in payment for sexual relations, and it was with the blood of a goat on Joseph's robe that the brothers deceived Jacob about Joseph's disappearance. (Earlier it was by ·wearing the skins of young goats that Jacob disguised himself and cheated Esau out of the patriarchal blessing.) When Tamar is about to be executed at the command of Judah she sends the items he had given in pledge, asking him to recognize them as his (hakker-nā? lemî..., 38.25), and Judah recognized (wayyakkēr) them. Earlier, in the betrayal of Joseph and deception of Jacob, the brothers asked Jacob whether he recognized the robe of Joseph (hakker-nā? hakketōnet

bin^ekā, 37.32), and he recognized it (wayyakkîrāh, 37.33).
The ironic theme of knowledge and recognition continues
with the story of Joseph and his brothers. When the brothers
later go down into Egypt for grain in time of famine, they
appear before Joseph.

> And Joseph saw his brothers and he recognized them
> [wayyakkirēm], but he acted as a stranger [wayyitnakkēr]
> to them and spoke harshly to them. And he said to them,
> "Where do come from?" and they said, "From the land of
> Canaan to buy food." And Joseph recognized [wayyakkēr]
> his brothers, but they did not recognize him [lō?
> hikkirûhû]. [42.7-8]

The theme is brought to a climax with the moving disclosure
scene in ch. 45: "and no one attended Joseph while he made
himself known (b^ehitwadda^c) to his brothers" (v. 1).

Judah, one of the leaders of the brothers, is lacking in
knowledge, lacking, indeed, in wisdom. His first son by an
anonymous canaanite woman marries Tamar and is "slain by
Yahweh" (38.7). The second son by the same woman then
marries Tamar, and he meets the same fate (38.10). Judah
seeks to avert the loss of more sons by deferring indefinitely
the giving of a third son as husband to Tamar, thus breaking
the levirate obligation to the dead brother's wife. Tamar then
takes matters into her own hands to rectify the wrong, and
Judah acts in a characteristic manner: blindly, without knowledge. When he sees Tamar sitting by the entrance of Enaim
("springs, eyes") he takes her to be a prostitute ("... for he
didn't know that she was his daughter-in-law"). Tamar's
aggressive action is abetted by Judah's sexual desire and
conventional expectations. He cannot see further than what
he desires, moved by personal passion rather than by commitment to Israel and the God of Israel. A change of heart
occurs only when he and the brothers are plunged into the
deprivation of famine and a worse calamity, the unutterable
grief of their father should he lose Benjamin as well as
Joseph. When Judah offers himself as a slave to Joseph in the
place of Benjamin (44.18-34), this precipitates the recognition scene in which Joseph reveals his identity.

Meanwhile, Tamar wins her case. Judah acknowledges that
she is in the right and he is not. Even though prostitution is
not countenanced in Israel's moral and legal traditions, and
although various kinds of dishonesty are continually cas-
tigated as contrary to human community, Tamar's deed is

accepted as rightful vindication. As Judah says, "She is more righteous than I" (38.26), i.e., she is vindicated and I am guilty.

Thus with Tamar we see how another "alien" person becomes part of Israel's identity. The narrator stays quietly in the wings. The effect of the adroit, matter of fact account is to give the impression that the implied author sees the divine hand in the course of complex human events. Judah's exogamous escapades lead to the predicament of Tamar. He has intercourse with Tamar, who he thinks is a "whore" (zônâ, 38.15), but whom he later tries to represent as a "cultic prostitute" (q^edēšâ, 38.21). We are not told whether Tamar is a canaanite woman, but in any event she brings home to him his guilt, which suggests also his culpability in the larger context of the Joseph story, and through an incestuous act (father and daughter-in-law) an ancestor of David is conceived. Through her righteous self-assertiveness, which involves disguise and deception, Tamar protects herself, enables her twins to survive, and mitigates Judah's guilt by bearing an ancestor of David.[6]

The stories of Deborah, Jael and Judith have all been reviewed at some length. They all have roles that are not simply linked to the fulfillment of a male's destiny. Deborah is a "mother in Israel," i.e., leader and prophet. Judith is beautiful and wise. Deborah, with Barak, leads Israel against the Canaanites and Judith sallies forth on her own to deceive the assyrian army commander. There is also more than a hint of counter-order in the narrative portraits of Esther and Mary. Esther is not autonomous in any sense, but her position as the foreign king's wife and her name, so obviously derived from Ishtar, suggest the foreign realities, both political and religious, that the Jews have had to come to terms with. Mary is a very passive figure in the early christian sources, but as a symbol of the christian arche-mother, beginning already with Luke's gospel, she discloses a dynamic tendency toward the understanding that she cannot simply belong to any human history. As virgin she is independent of human males, being married only to the divine "father."

However, none of these figures, including Tamar, is a fully articulated representation of counter-order. Mary is independent of human males, but functions only in relation to the divine Father and Son. The others all use feminine means and scenarios which depict the downfall of males through the "weakness" of woman. That is, the normal low social and political status of women is a precondition of the meaning of the stories. Eve and Ruth are the two exceptions to this pattern.

The prevailing interpretation of Eve throughout the generations in Judaism and Christianity is that her weakness led to Adam's sin, and indeed that she was a temptress. The earliest jewish articulation of this point of view as definite doctrine in an extant text is found in Sirach 25.21-24 (heb. vv. 20-23): "From a woman the beginning of iniquity ...." (heb. v. 23a). In other words, the docrinal hardening of such a view may be dated to the early second century B.C., although an element of misogyny is apparent in the earlier wisdom tradition.

In fact, when one reads Proverbs closely there is not much to be found that could clearly be called misogynous. The reflections on the alien woman indicate a sense of danger which lies in the feminine, but, as already discussed, the zārâ is a metaphor of seductive speech. By contrast, there are proverbs favorable to women (e.g., 11.16; 19.14), and those that are derogatory caricatures are no more searing (e.g., 11.22; 19.13; 27.16) than many proverbial pictures of men. For a truly misogynous statement one must look to Kohelet (7.26-28), ca. 300-250 BC. Even with Kohelet, however, there is not a consistently anti-feminine attitude, as we see in his poetic portrayal of the desirability of enjoying one's "portion," which includes the joy of "life with the woman you love" (9.9).

One may wonder whether the penetration of hellenistic cultural influence in the 3rd century BC was a factor in the hardening of myths and teachings that could tend to misogyny. (On greek wisdom concerning the danger represented by women, see Carlston: 95.) We know, of course, that the division of women into seductive harlot and the faithful wife and mother goes far back in ancient near eastern cultural history. The egyptian Ptahhotep (ca. 2450 BC) presents the image of woman as a seductress, as like painted porcelain, like a dream; she is the agent of death (Pritchard: 413). In a satirical akkadian text, "the Dialogue of Pessimism," from the second millennium BC, woman is imaged as a well or pit (Pritchard: 438). These are images which older biblical wisdom employs, but in the jewish tradition the blaming of woman for the sinful condition of the world becomes a crystallized teaching only in the hellenistic period.

But to return to the garden story, in more recent exegesis some interpreters (e.g., Trible) have held that the contrary is the case: the text tells a tale of the superiority of the woman, who is the active, intelligent one in the temptation scene, and is certainly not depicted as a "temptress." Moreover, it is fallacious to hold that the woman is subordinate because she is fashioned from the man. By this logic it would follow that the man is subordinate to the soil because he is made from it. The contrary is true in the pre-transgression phase of the story. It is more accurate to say that the woman is co-ordinate. She is a new element in the man's life by which he knows himself as "ʾîs," "male." She is from him and yet other than he. She is described in the peculiar expression "Cēzer keneḡdô," "helpmate" (Gen 2.20), literally "a help before him" or "contrary to him." The meaning is apparently that of "complement," that which completes, fills a lack. The man's function is first of all to care for the ground and its plants. Now he will cleave to the woman, becoming "one flesh" with her (2.24).

In short, Eve is a figure embodying an aspect of human being that Adam lacks. His maleness and his "seed" (children) can come about only through her, and she has an active intelligence. The only creature in the tale not formed from the earth, she is the mediatrix between the man and the serpent, interpreting the cunning creature's overtures in the best way that her naiveté would allow.

When the three characters are punished according to their individual origin and function, the woman is made subordinate to the man, just as the man loses his full partnership with the soil But even in her subordination the man names her "ḥavvâ," "because she was/is the mother of all living."

Concerning Ruth, we have already seen that the plot of the story involves a reversal of the primary elements of the typic scene of the betrothal, a reversal that represents the feminine figure as the foreigner who takes the initiative and the masculine figure as the one who engages in a form of deception (concealment of facts) in order to mediate between world and protagonist.

One of the most interesting aspects of the story is that Ruth's explicit motive in journeying to Judah is simply loyalty to Naomi; there is nothing of a divine call and promise, although the knowledgable reader would catch the allusion to Abraham's journey in Boaz's first conversation with Ruth (2.11). As already noted, Boaz's blessing upon her opens a network of allusions that is important in understanding the tale (2.12). Ruth is not called by Yahweh, but in coming to Judah she seeks shelter "under his wings." Wings of refuge is a very feminine image, that of a mother bird. It appears in some of the psalms that speak of safety and protection in the shadow or shelter of God's wings (Ps 36.8; 57.2; 61.5; 91.4). That is, Ruth has come to Yahweh as to a mother.

The concrete manifestation of this divine maternal protection will be the acts of Boaz. When Boaz awakes and discovers Ruth lying beside him on the threshing floor, he is startled - as well he might be, for he had lain down with a "merry heart" from the evening's feasting (3.7) and it was very dark. Ruth asks him to spread the wing of his skirt over her, "for you are redeemer" (3.9). That is, he is the near kinsman who can buy Elimelech's land and marry her.

Ruth's loyalty to Naomi revives the latter in her old age. As the women sing,

for your daughter-in-law, who loves you, has borne him, she who is better to you than seven sons. [4.15]

The extraordinary nature of Ruth's loyalty is affirmed as better than having many sons. The narrative thus recognizes the exceptional nature of what has transpired. Of course, it could be viewed as only exceptional, that is, the character of Ruth is a one-time thing, and so no conclusion concerning the meaning of Israel should be drawn from it. But the structure and dynamic of the story pull one to the view that the author had a definite agenda. The use of ancient israelite story patterns and images and the place of Ruth as ancestress of David suggest that something essential is being said about the people Israel. Whether or not the book of Ruth was intended to speak to a specific historical and social situation, such as the problem of intermarriage and identity in postexilic Judah, it certainly communicates that an essential dimension of Israel is the foreign feminine east (from which Abraham came), and that divine providence may work in a quiet "motherly" fashion.

There is a depth, a mystery about Eve in Gen 2-3 and Ruth in the book of Ruth in spite of the classical simplicity of the hebrew prose style, which gives the impression of a naive world view. Both are images of dimensions of Israel's identity which stand as constant reminders even when they are ignored or overinterpreted in modes of seeing that admit only the importance of patriarchal heroes. Eve is the primal wife-mother on whom Adam depends and who deals with the enigmatic "foreign" power embodied in the serpent. Ruth is, among other things, the feminine representation of Israel's connection with the "foreign east" from which it came.

Excursus: Hagar

I stated, in chapter II, that Hagar is an image of another order; in fact, however, she is an ambiguous in-between character in the Genesis narratives. As will be apparent in the following discussion of the alien woman, she does not fit in the category of negative counter-order because she is Sarah's servant, given to Abraham, and she receives a divine promise analogous to the one given to Abraham (Gen 16.10). Though her son will be "wild" (16.12), he is to become the father of great nation (21.18). Yet Hagar is foreign, an Egyptian. She belittles Sarah when she conceives, and she is unable in her predicament to help her son (21.15-16). It is God who directly intervenes in the wilderness of Beersheba to save the two of them. At the end of the second tale she matches Ishmael with a wife from Egypt (21.21). Thus Hagar does not act contrary to the reality of Israel, being rather mistreated herself. Yet she is Egyptian and contemptuous of Sarah. She is ancestress of the Ishmaelites, yet cannot act effectively as mediating agent as does the israelite arche-mother. She is a reminder in the larger story of origins that Israel moves among the peoples and is related to Egypt and Ishmael - but not so closely as to threaten the unity achieved in Abraham and Sarah through Isaac.

2. The Alien Woman

The alien woman is the temptress. Her essential characteristic in the three clearly drawn narrative personages is that she uses seductive speech to attempt to lead the hero away from his vocation for Israel, or, as related in Proverbs, she seduces the man away from order to anarchy, the life of a fool. She has nothing to do with Israel's origins, she is "foreign," functioning as a metaphor in the wisdom literature. She portrays one who mediates a destiny contrary to the divine purpose by her way of linking language and sex.

Gen 39 is a crucial episode in the Joseph story. If he succumbs to the blandishments of Potiphar's wife, then Israel is undone. The narrator arrives at the text's goal in the disclosure scene: "God sent me before you for preservation of life" (Gen 45.5). Joseph did not die when cast in the pit by his brothers, but now the egyptian woman is another "pit." Even though he refuses to be tempted, her false accusation lands him in prison, still another kind of "pit." Joseph was indeed "brought down to Egypt" (hûrad miṣrāy^{e}mâ, 39.1) in having been betrayed by his brothers, subjected to sexual enticement and imprisoned. But even in prison "Yahweh was with him" (39.23).

Joseph is endangered in spite of himself (though there is more than a hint of his self-obsessed vanity as the story begins). Samson's downfall occurs because of himself. There are intimations of trouble to come from the announcement of Samson's birth, as we have observed in ch. III. His various antics are in keeping with the image of fire that informs the Samson tales (Ju 14.15; 15.4-8, 14): it is "a metonymic image of Samson himself: a blind, uncontrolled force, leaving a terrible swath of destruction behind it ...." (Alter: 95) Thus the philistine Delilah apparently faces no great challenge in coaxing Samson's secret out of him. That it proves to be quite a task after all is partially accounted for by the riddling character of the final episode. Suspense is built up and Samson's great stupidity is shown through the accumulation of questions and answers. But the nature of his answers touches on a second factor - undisciplined as his urges are, Samson is still protected by the divine power within him due to his avowed vocation. External bonds cannot hold him. But when the woman cajoles and harasses him to the point that he betrays the nazirite vow made by his mother for him, he is completely vulnerable to his foes. When his seven locks of hair are shaved off the Philistines capture him and put his eyes out. His final blindness is a concrete condition in the narrative which confirms his spiritual condition all along.

The temptress in Proverbs corresponds generally to what is depicted of Potiphar's wife and Delilah except that she is not represented in relation to Israel's national traditions. She leads the man away from the "paths of life" (Prov 2.19). Dame Wisdom, however, possesses "paths of peace" (3.17), inviting humans to her (1.20f.). She is even involved in the very structure of creation itself (8.22-31). As such her symbolic functions are very similar to those of the arche-mother and are the corrective to the ways of the woman who is "zārâ" and "nokriyyâ," "foreign, alien."

Yet there are many instances in which an arche-mother and other heroines act deceitfully or use lying language. How are they related to the shadow figure of the alien woman? This will be taken up in the next chapter.

In conclusion, the woman as counter-order represents great ambiguity with respect to the symbolic functions of the arche-mother, and in the form of the alien woman she contradicts them. The positive feminine figures of counter-order include Leah and Tamar, who are unloved but who exhibit considerable initiative and who bear significant sons. Deborah and Judith are militant women who are the objects of love and inspiration and who protect their people, but they are not connected to a particular male or the birth of a hero. Esther likewise is a beauty desired by others and a mediatrix for her people, but she is not a figure of origins and nurture. Mary does not have a mediating function in the NT gospels and the gospel of James. But she is the mother of a savior, she is the object of love and inspiration, and like Esther she has a story in her own right.

Eve and Ruth are the most unusual of the positive figures of counter-order. Eve is a coincidence of opposites who is the mother of the ?ādām from which she comes, the man's object of wonder ("At last! Bone of my bones," etc.) whom he will subject, and the mediatrix of a knowledge that will bring ?ādām both godlike wisdom and the suffering of primary alienation. Ruth becomes a mother, but Naomi is the real source of nurture in the story. Ruth is the object of Boaz's admiration, but she comes to his attention due to her initiative, and it is Boaz who fully initiates her into the israelite world. If she mediates anything, it is Israel's recovery of its sense of its own origins, its own "otherness" in the foreign feminine east.

As for the temptress, she seeks to lead the chosen one into a false anti-world, into the contradiction of God's order. Potiphar's wife would seduce Joseph into the disorder of a false Egypt. Samson is undone by Philistines through Delilah. And the alien woman of proverbs is the agent of social and moral anarchy. All three use the power of language to conceal and to distort meanings in order to lead the man away from his proper path.

Chapter V

THE BIBLICAL FEMININE AND
CONTEMPORARY RELIGIOUS THOUGHT

A. Review of Results

I BEGAN this study with a discussion of our point of view and method in reading texts. The essential element in both perspective and methodology has been the thesis that biblical narrative represents a dynamic mode of thinking, of communicating and arriving at knowledge. Narrative is a mode of expression that weaves a sequence of events from beginning to end through a middle. This "middle" involves conflict, lack, or testing, and a movement toward resolution of the problem. It builds a world, whether large or limited, whether referring to the real or the imagined, and it proceeds through a temporal continuum. The features of world construction and narrated time are among the main points of contrast with aphoristic discourse, which is a non-narrative mode of reflection that represents the timeless. Aphorism is a genre of transition or conflict as it offers glimpses into small aspects of an accepted order of things or seeks to move between contraries of experience and thought to a new vision of things.

As a form of thinking, biblical narrative is dramatic, experientially oriented, and replete with thematically interwoven images and metaphors. It functions as a way of "thinking upon" (reflecting) and "thinking of" (remembering, caring, discovering) as it tells Israel who she is and continually reraises the question of identity. Our initial critical guide was Robert Alter. His perceptive essays on biblical narrative treat it as a process, as a pioneering technique of prose fiction which is a way of expressing and knowing the ever shifting, always tenuous, but God-guided history of Israel. Two other critics were cited whose approaches support and enrich this essay. Frank Kermode distinguishes "myth" and "fiction" in terms of their handling of closure, experiential stability, and autocriticism. ("If we forget that fictions are fictive we regress to myth" [Kermode: 41]). Herbert Schneidau argues that biblical "historicized fiction," with its predilection for parataxis and metonymy (sequential ordering and suggesting one name or image by using another, associated one), is fundamentally different from cosmological myth with its hierarchical analogies and correspondences. Kermode's views can be applied only mutatis mutandis to biblical literature, and Schneidau is not precise enough in his categorizations, but both offer orienting insights that supplement Alter's.

The concrete textual support of the thesis is located in the stories in which women are central figures. Not all women in biblical literature were selected, but those whose functions are closely tied to Israel's origins and destiny. The point of departure was the "arche-mother" ("beginning" or "model mother"). The Genesis mothers, Sarah, Rebecca, and Rachel, are determinative in this ideal characterization, but the mother of Moses, the egyptian princess, Zipporah, the mother of Samson and Hannah also enter into the composite picture. The tales of these feminine personages were read as instances of a subtle and supple prose fiction in which the artistic ordering of key words (Leitwörter), speeches, and recurring events plays a crucial role.

The arche-mother was interpreted as a primary representation of Israel's being in the world. She is an aspect of Israel as a new order of God. Starting from four kinds of typic scene - betrothal, wife as sister, agon, and promise to the barren wife - we found her to be the source of progeny and nurture, and at the same time a great beauty desired by others besides the patriarch. She is thus continually endangered in a variety of circumstances that are of a "type": a foreign ruler tries to possess her, often abetted by the patriarch, but the God of the ancestors intervenes, obtrusively or inobtrusively, in order to deliver her and the father from the predicament. As it turns out, they emerge from the predicament wealthier than before. She protects the chosen one and in some cases enables him to begin the process of realizing his destiny. As for the promises and the journey of faith, she is not as closely related to the God as the ancestor, but she is simultaneously more able to divert the menacing powers of the "world" (father, king, god) that threaten the male hero.

With the arche-mother as the reference, we looked at a

number of women whose narrative portrayals differ in varying degrees from her:

1.   Eve, "the mother of all living." The key to understanding her is the representation of the coincidence of opposites. She is "woman" and individual (Eve), the mother and daughter of Adam, as well as the mate (ʔiššâ) of Adam insofar as he is male (ʔîš). The only creature not made directly from the ground, she is an intelligent but naive interpreter of the divine prohibition. She is not a temptress - there is nothing of that in Gen 3 - but she is the one whom the serpent, the "foreign" beast, approaches, and she gives her rather passive mate some of the fruit to eat.

2.   Deborah, Jael and Judith, the aggressive or warrior woman. All three function directly and aggressively against a foreign power outside of the family circle, in contradistinction to the arche-mother. Deborah has the socio-religious roles of judge and prophet; Judith overrides the advice of her town's elders and conceives her own plan to save Israel. She and Jael both slay the commanding officer of the enemy troops. However, the narrator has cast an overarching, "womanly" net over all three. Deborah's role is characterized as that of a "mother in Israel," Jael serves as the proper hostess in deceiving Sisera, Judith captivates Holofernes and captures his head with her beauty as well as clever speech.

3.   Esther and Mary, the dependent heroine. Contrary to Eve and the warrior woman, neither Esther nor Mary speaks or acts out of her own personal center. Neither is a "self-starter." Mary is especially passive. Yet both have significant parts to play. Esther is the mate of the foreign king due to her beauty, and as such she is in a position to save her people. Mary gives birth to the christian savior, and eventually becomes the arche-mother for Christianity in a mythical sense (a development already well on its way in the gospel of James, about 150 AD). Both are the subjects of historicized fictions (book of Esther, gospel of James), as is Judith. Mary is passive, but she is "independent" to the extent that her role is realized primarily in relation to God, not her human husband.

4.   Ruth, the woman as antipatriarch (i.e., reversal of the patriarchal perspective). In Ruth most of the components of the betrothal typic scene are reversed, placing Ruth, her relation to Naomi, and her origins in the forefront. She is a foreigner (Moabite), one from the east who journeys to a land and people she did not know (cf. Abraham) out of loyalty to

her mother-in-law. She takes refuge under Yahweh's <u>wings</u> and subsequently takes the initiative in asking Boaz to cover her with his <u>skirt-wings</u>. The story ends with Naomi nursing the baby of Ruth and Boaz, a son who is the ancestor of David.

5.   Potiphar's wife, Delilah, and the alien woman in Proverbs: the temptress. The temptress is a seductress. The medium of her seductive wiles is deceitful and distorted language. In the stories of Joseph and Samson she tries to tempt the hero away from his vocation for Israel, abetted in the case of Samson by the hero's undisciplined nature and practical stupidity. In Proverbs she leads the man away from discipline and right social order. Tamar appears at first to belong to this picture, but she seeks simply to redress the wrong done her by Judah, and her "seduction" of Judah is accomplished thanks to his blind male assumptions (true also of Sisera and Holofernes). But the figure of Tamar, as well as Judith, does suggest an important point: the heroine herself, including the arche-mother, often acts deceitfully, deluding even the patriarch. In other words, the features of the arche-mother and other heroines overlap those of the temptress.

The arche-mother performs symbolic functions as the progenitress, the object of love and inspiration, and agent of change for the hero, enabling him to move successfully into the world or actually determining his destiny. In these functions, especially as mediatrix between world and hero, her acts and character are reminiscent of the mythical feminine. The mediating functions of the arche-mother are absent, or are aligned to different ends in the accounts of other women who intimate a counter-order, another kind of centering of life and thought than found in the arche-mother. These other women are the images of other dimensions, sometimes an "underside," in the narrative thinking of Israel. Most of them are presented as positive variations or contraries of the order embodied in the arche-mother. Leah is not beautiful and is unloved, yet she is the mother of six of the tribes and her servant bears two other sons of Israel. Tamar plays the harlot to win her rights, and gives birth to Perez, ancestor of David. The stories of Deborah, Jael, and Judith are not tied to a specific male's destiny. The two most striking figures of positive counter-order are Eve and Ruth. Eve represents a coincidence of opposites - belonging to Adam as human, other than he as female; source of man who

113

is her "matter," she is the mediatrix between the man and the serpent, interpreting the serpent's animal cunning in a manner betraying her intelligent naïveté. Ruth is a mirror of Israel's origin, a foreigner from the east who travels to an unknown land with a mother-in-law she loves. She is received by Yahweh, according to Boaz's interpretation, and by Boaz, according to Ruth's request, as a mother bird spreading her wings over her young.

The negative figures of counter-order are contradictions from the standpoint of Israel's thinking about its identity and its world. That is, they contradict the new, divinely given order in history. If Potiphar's wife had succeeded in seducing Joseph, there might have been no Israel. Samson's downfall at the hands (or tongue!) of Delilah shows, according to Judges, how tenuously the charismatic leaders held things together after Joshua. These women try to tempt the hero into a foreign reality; they are therefore false objects of love and inspiration. Likewise the alien woman of Proverbs: she is a continual reminder of chaos in the form of abusing the potential of language, disregarding one's elders (or tradition), and leading a life of moral folly.

Two topics now remain to be treated. One is a question which I have touched upon frequently without having directly addressed it: what is the relation of the "feminine," sexuality and language in Israel's narrative thinking? The other is what this study implies for contemporary theology.

B. The Feminine, Sexuality and Language

In pondering the meaning of the "feminine" in the context of this book I shall deal with two related but distinct areas. In a brief ontological analysis of the human condition the "feminine" will be clarified on the basis of some primary experiences universally connected with the feminine sex. This does not mean that every human without remainder has had all of these experiences, but that they may reasonably be considered universal, typical in human experience. As primary and universal they may be so elementary that they tell us little about the specific symbolic expressions of a given culture, but they offer at least a point of departure in our reflections. The second area will be our emerging set of ideas concerning how women are actually understood in the narrative thinking of Israel's origins, destiny, and distinctive way in the world. Israel's faith is a dynamic faith in a transcendent, covenant God who guides his people through an ever-shifting, ambiguous and dangerous history which reflects humankind's state of exile (Gen 3.22-4.16) and fragmentation (Gen 11.1-9). Our thesis is that the universal, ontological sense of the feminine is actualized in the biblical images of woman in accordance with this faith.

The essential oppositions[1] of existence stem from the awareness of self and other. "Self" is the knowledge one has of being "this" center, this personal being distinct from others, from "world." The self-other awareness of human being is a kind of structure, a dynamic structure in which the self seeks to be itself, but also to participate in the other; to assert its freedom, yet attain to a meaningful end (telos) which is not simply a self-created, arbitrary goal; to enhance its growth, yet maintain the forms necessary for continuity and survival. (See Tillich: 168-86.) These tensions of the self-other relation are the precondition of language. Language presupposes the relation of self and other, which it grounds, and the distance between them, which it seeks to bridge.

One of the primary modes of concretely expressing the self-other awareness is sexuality, because the content of the self and the other is so powerfully charged and formed by sexual roles and drives from the cradle to the grave. The realizing of selfhood in relation to whatever world one inhabits must include being born, sexual identification, and perpetuating the species. Here, to repeat, we are considering universal patterns, to which there have been and are obvious exceptions in given cultural settings. Whatever the truth about cultural conditioning in sexuality may be, it seems that for both males and females certain facts are universal.

1. Everyone must be born of woman (so far, although "brave new worlds" à la Huxley have been envisaged).
2. Everyone must be succored as an infant. For most humans this is done by their birth-mother. This fact is of significance in the association of the feminine with psychosocial development.
3. The female receives or takes the male seed into her body.

Outside of any other facts or any world views, these aspects of human existence constitute the necessary condition for making the female the accessible "matter" for symbolic fashioning of ideas of the feminine that have prevailed in actual historical life. The female is the one who carries and bears the infant, and she brings about transition from fetal life to fully human life. She nourishes and nurtures the child. As the recipient of the male semen she brings about the transition from "life" (seed) to fetus.

Now sexuality, in turn, suggests the oppositions "life and death." With the emergence of the self, the self knows it will "die" if it is separated from the "other." The other - mother, then father, immediate environment and larger world - is needed for physical and psychical survival. No other, no self. But human survival is impossible without meaning, so self and world must acknowledge and signify each other. If there is no other, there is neither any sense of the self in the first place nor anything to signify. A sign given by the self is already a sign of the other. In this self-other dialectic that is rooted in being and the threat of not being, sexuality is the most pressing constant reminder of life and death. Sexuality is formed and informed by roles, and these roles are in turn permeated with ideas and assumptions about masculinity and femininity. The sexual drive is that power whereby the gen- erations are generated, but generations, by definition, pass away. One is son/daughter in relation to mother/father and other ancestors living and dead. Within the larger context of a person's life one is required to give up childhood to assume the roles, including the sexual life, of adulthood. If one has children, they must be given up, so to say. That is, the parent-child relation is also part of the round of change whose perimeters are appearance and disappearance. So it is that one must die as part of the process of the generations.

There are other aspects of sexuality that may be culture-specific. If a certain tradition is rigidly set against "loss of control,"[2] then sexual passion and intercourse may intimate loss of vitality and pollution.

The role of the feminine, it is fair to say, has been traditionally and universally that of bring about the self- other awareness and of mediating the conflicts and obstacles between self and other. The feminine has stood between the person and the world with respect to psychosocial de- velopment. The feminine is connected to extending oneself through family (the generations) and enabling the self to be realized in the world. In other words, the feminine figure characteristically leads from other (or world) to the self and from self to the world.

These functions of the feminine persona have certainly been common in the american cultural heritage as reflected in its literature. Anne Bradstreet, our first woman poet and the first notable white poet on these shores, viewed her poetic work as a kind of childbearing and mothering. In a poem prefacing the second edition of her collected poems, published posthumously, she writes of her little book as of a child, albeit a strange infant, either bastard or virgin-born:

> If for thy Father askt, say, thou hadst none:
> And for thy Mother, she alas is poor,
> Which caused her thus to send thee out of door.

Sarah Edwards served Jonathan Edwards as a kind of buffer and protector, taking care of daily household and other matters. Written accounts say that her great beauty was a source of delight to her husband, and she served as his primary model of authentic religious experience. (See Porterfield: 39-45.)

Emily Dickinson, entrapped in a predicament of unorthodox religious sensibilites, poetic genius without an audience, and social and temperamental isolation, sought a new view of herself that would transcend the bounds of puritan, patriarchal presuppositions. This new, "queenly" self she saw as divine (#458), a kind of female God:

> A solemn thing - it was - I said
> A woman - white - to be -
> And wear - if God should count me fit -
> Her blameless mystery -   [#271]

> Title divine - is mine!
> The wife - without the sign!
> Acute Degree - conferred on me -
> Empress of Calvary -   [#1072]

Yet the "eyes" of the uncompassionate puritan God looked upon her. These eyes are a blank, a wilderness which is inhospitable to the female poet:

> Like Eyes that looked on Wastes -
> Incredulous of Ought
> But Blank - and steady Wilderness -
> Diversified by Night -   [#458]

She seems to have imagined the way from the old self vis-à-vis the Unreceptive Other to the new self as through a network of experiences formed by feminine metaphors of disorder, i.e., antichristian metaphors, which for her were practically synonymous with antipuritan. For example, the

117

metaphor of the witch and the temptress. The witch is Dickinson's psychopomp to a new sense of identity.

I think I was enchanted
When first a sombre girl -
I read that Foreign Lady -
The Dark - felt beautiful -
* * * * * * * *
'Tis Antidote to turn -

To tomes of solid Witchcraft -
Magicians be asleep -
But Magic - hath an Element
Like Deity to keep -   [#593]

"Witchcraft" is a recurring image of the quotidian power that not only manifests itself in beauty (#776), but allows the poetess to function day by day and work as an artist.

Witchcraft was hung, in History,
But History and I
Find all the witchcraft that we need
Around us every day.   [#1583]

Some feminine mediators do not perform their traditional function, so from the standpoint of the hero's goals the story aborts. In Fitzgerald's "The Great Gatsby" Daisy's unwillingness and inability to be Gatsby's alter, his other half, as he tries to enter into the upper class american world of his fantasies symbolizes his unsuccessful quest and his death. As Nick the narrator muses at the end of the novel,

... I thought of Gatsby's wonder when he first picked out the green light at the end of Daisy's dock. He had come a long way to this blue lawn, and his dream must have seemed so close that he could hardly fail to grasp it ....
Gatsby believed in the green light, the orgiastic future that year by year recedes before us.   [Fitzgerald: 182]

On the other hand, some of the women in Hawthorne's short stories (Faith, Beatrice, Georgiana) represent the possibility of transition into another realm, which the male protagonist denies. In "The Scarlet Letter" Hester Prynne meets Arthur Dimmesdale in the forest and attempts to entice him into the vision of a new being.

Begin all anew! .... The future is yet full of trial and success .... give up this name of Arthur Dimmesdale, and make thyself another, and a high one ....   [170]

118

However, he cannot handle the transformation process. He becomes a "new man," but one which must die.

Another man had returned out of the forest; a wiser one; with a knowledge of hidden mysteries which the simplicity of the former never could have reached. A bitter kind of knowledge that! [191]

The mediating function of the feminine in many symbolic texts and contexts is closely related to the function of language, that of mediating self and world to each other. Language as the precondition of humanness both presupposes a distance between self and other and a relationship that can be established or confirmed. Being "in" language and using language is to be born into humanity. One is raised in it and by it. Language receives and refashions new human experiences and artifacts. Language is both an artifact itself and a repertory for arranging reality that is prior to all artifacts. In the latter sense "language" is not essentially words, but the principles and paradigms whereby words are arranged and made to mean something. My formula will be then:

Language is the primary presupposition and mediation of self and other, sexuality is the human experience of oppositions most closely tied to the self-other functioning of language.

Feminine sexuality has been one of the chief elements in primary experience which are available to symbolize the interface or boundary of the self-world relationship.

To turn to the specific religious and literary matrix of the Bible, the feminine personages of Scripture have a key role in mediating "world" to males and yet enabling them to distance themselves from attachment to the cosmic forces and cosmological civilizations that would keep them from the service of the One who transcends all stories and all names. They are buffers, protectors, defenders, and nourishers. It is Eve whom the serpent approaches and who endeavors to assess his argument concerning the forbidden fruit. Sarah stands between the foreign king and what Abraham perceives as certain death for himself unless she protects him. Moses's mother gives him a lease on life and nurses him due to the compassion of the royal egyptian woman! Deborah, Jael and Judith act militantly and militarily to defend their people. Some of these women mediate knowledge - the knowledge of good and evil (Eve) and the knowledge of destiny (Rebecca). They enable the chosen one to surmount obstacles to his destiny in order that Israel may be and the Israel of the future may be formed.

How, then, do the ancient jewish arche-mother and other biblical feminine types observed in this study[3] differ from the mythical feminine of other traditions? We have taken note of the "harlot lass" in the Gilgamesh epic, Anat's deeds on Baal's behalf in the Baal cycle, Paghat's quest to find her brother's murderer in the tale of Aqhat, and Dame Wisdom as psychopomp in Proverbs and Wisdom. Among many other figures one could mention the Virgin as mediatrix in medieval Christianity (Watts: 102, 110). The difference is that the israelite females are ordinary humans depicted usually as definite individuals, but who belong to the extraordinary story of a people and its God, whose story is that of his world and his people. They are neither divine nor objects of worship or veneration nor (with the exception of Deborah) bearers of a special religious vocation. Their roles arise out of the kaleidoscopic narrative order that leads always to a new stage in the quest to create and preserve the new humanity called Israel. They bear the new seed in history, they serve the God of no time and no place, they belong to the possibility of a new people and a new language after Babel. All the more reason that they cannot represent a numinous power in and of themselves or be associated with cultic practices. Since only God and God's word endure, the woman, as the link between the chosen one and the world, must disappear. Her divinely favored offspring will be tested and can never see the dénouement of the odyssey of Israel - Jacob and Joseph die in Egypt, Moses is not permitted to enter the land of Canaan, Samuel dies when an unwanted monarchy has emerged.[4] As the hero is limited in his vocation to the "not yet," to the other side of the Jordan, so to speak, so also the heroine's function must cease to exist in the narrative flow which begins and ends in the mystery of the God whose reality is revealed but always refracted through a glass darkly.

She may be a deceiver insofar as she stands for Israel against the world, which characteristically takes the form of hostile male powers, whether husband and older son (Rebecca/Isaac, Esau), father (Rachel/Laban), father and king (mother of Moses, egyptian princess/pharaoh), army commander (Jael/Sisera; Judith/Holofernes), or royal counselor

(Esther/Haman). In the salvation history the woman becomes a temptress only as an "alien" who seeks to seduce the hero away from Israel, when she uses cunning speech to try to delude the hero and take him into the kind of sexuality that would strip him of his divinely conferred calling (Potiphar's wife/Joseph; Delilah/Samson). As far as the pre-Apocrypha wisdom tradition is concerned, she is not related to Israel per se. Israel and Israel's sacred story do not figure directly in the wisdom writings until Sirach in the Apocrypha (ca. 180 BC). In Proverbs the alien woman uses the complex relation of disclosure and concealment, the said and unsaid that is built into language in order to become the agent of disorder. She lures the male from autonomy (or theonomy in a broad sense) to entrapment in passions, from stable society to anarchy.

The exception to many of these conclusions is the book of Ruth. Except for the narrative frame, which begins and ends in a conventional patriarchal mode (1.1-2; 4.17-22),[5] the roles of male and female are reversed. The foreign woman comes from her own land to Judah, a journey compared by allusion to Abraham's. She takes the initiative in a sexually daring act that leads to betrothal, but it is the male who then mediates between her and the world. Boaz acts according to social and legal conventions in order to accomplish the marriage. It is he who wishes to conceal something due to social conventions (3.14), and he cleverly manipulates the legal situation so that he can take Ruth as his wife without alienating the two of them from their society. This charming and unusual little piece of fiction implies an author who is working out a new - or renewed - understanding of Israel and perhaps of himself or herself.

In conclusion, the feminine in biblical narrative functions in a manner similar to the part language plays as a repertory of patterns and symbols that reveal and conceal meanings. It is thus no accident that language could be imaged as a woman (Prov 18.21) and in her positive functions she is one aspect of Dame Wisdom in Proverbs. The key feminine personage is, from the perspective assumed here, that aspect of humanness turned toward the world and that part of the world turned toward the human. I am speaking of symbolic functions, of course, for every actual female is in a complex of self-other relations. It is simply that our paradigmatic accounts exhibit a certain kind of role for the symbolic reality of the feminine. As, for instance, Eve and Adam: not only does the serpent approach the woman with a question about the tree to which she responds -

Adam/Eve ⟶ Serpent
response to question

but Eve then "communicates" the result to the man, thus going from serpent to man -

Adam ⟵ Eve/Serpent
fruit of knowledge

Likewise Sarah is between Abraham and the king of Egypt:

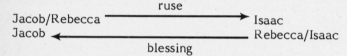

Abraham/Sarah ⟶ Egypt
sister (survival)
Abraham ⟵ Sarah/Egypt
wealth

And Jacob, Rebecca, and Isaac:

Jacob/Rebecca ⟶ Isaac
ruse
Jacob ⟵ Rebecca/Isaac
blessing

Or Judith, Israel, and Holofernes:

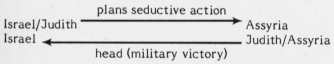

Israel/Judith ⟶ Assyria
plans seductive action
Israel ⟵ Judith/Assyria
head (military victory)

Ruth and Boaz are the exception to the pattern:

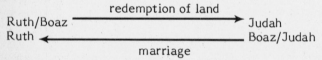

Ruth/Boaz ⟶ Judah
redemption of land
Ruth ⟵ Boaz/Judah
marriage

So also one can conceive and imagine in poetic figures the ordering and disordering power of language as it moves out from the "self" to the "world" in order to present something, ask something, command something, deceive, etc., and as it returns with what the world has to offer or what can be taken and assimilated. But the world wants also to speak to the self, so language is not only between self and world, it is necessary to both in any human sense. If in certain texts and a certain kind of thinking images of the feminine are so closely associated with the mediating role that language has, the implication would be that the experience of a necessary reality is depicted in the feminine forms; without this necessary reality there would be no human world.

C. Implications for Modern Theology

1. Interpretation of the Biblical Feminine

In interpreting the biblical feminine I have presumed all along that any sort of reductionism would miss the mark of meaning. That is, whatever meaning, whatever signification or pointing up of signs we may find, it cannot be reduced to any sort of literalism, to historical context, to underlying structures, or to literary forms. To be sure, my approach and methodology have been literary, but I understand "literary" in such a way that if offers an entrée into religious values and theological interpretation. I understand Scripture as divinely inspired, and for that reason I hold that it cannot be the primary object of faith. Only God is the object - and subject - of faith.[6] This is not to say there are no other inspired works, but that for Jews the Hebrew Scriptures and for Christians the Old Testament and New Testament are the central symbolic texts witnessing to the Source and End of all things.

What I say therefore in this part of the book will be of little interest unless the reader is already drawn to the question of how the Bible may be a mirror in which to see ourselves.

Now one of the things that must be most striking about this study is the multiplicity of images of the feminine. Even the arche-mother that I have sketched as an interpretive construct must finally be seen as artificial in relation to the great individuality that some of the biblical women exhibit through the common narrative patterns. What I have inferred, in effect, is that there is no one concrete picture of the feminine in the bible, although the composite picture of the arche-mother has been taken as a helpful point of departure and reference. Her beauty, her travail, and her mediating functions have been employed as clues both to the meaning of the feminine and of Israel in the biblical stories. The other women who represent in varying degrees either divergence or counter-order show how this general picture of the feminine may be expanded, transcended (Eve as coincidence of opposites), reversed (Ruth as the subject of faith's journey), and contradicted (the temptress as anti-Israel and anarchy).

123

This kaleidoscope of the feminine does not exist in some suspended state without context; it comes out of a history into our history. With respect to the biblical history, there were several historical situations and crises that informed the historicity of the biblical authors and to which the interpreter has to attend. The pre-Canaan period of "semi-nomadic" existence has left its mark. The struggle of Israel to establish itself in the land is another, as on the one hand Israel's identity was centered in seminomadic values and covenant with a guiding God, and on the other the practices and institutions of agrarian life and kingship were required for survival. The determinative event and situation was of course the babylonian exile, which, with the covenant tradition, gave rise to a sense of historicity that undergirded a total <u>imaginative structure</u> for understanding, assimilating, thematizing and fashioning the national story. From the "exile" of humankind from Eden, through the wanderings of the ancestors in and out of the promised land, to the conclusion of the Torah story east of the Jordan, exile as a way of viewing Israel vis-à-vis God and other peoples is a continual point of orientation for thought and imagination. Even with Israel in the land from Joshua through II Kings, the possibility of losing the land is an implied or explicit refrain as we read in the difficulties under the judges, through the struggle against the Philistines and the assyrian conquest of Israel and subjugation of Judah, to the babylonian deportation at the end of II Kings.

Within this total picture of the national history, with the exile symbolically centering the sense of detachment from the great civilizations characterized by cosmological ·myth, the arche-mother represents the possibility of losing the beauty of Israel to foreign powers, yet simultaneously the means by which Israel's distinctiveness, its chosenness, is protected through grace, beauty and wisdom. But she is not only "between" Israel and foreign powers - she is also often depicted as the agent for resolving Israel's own inner contradictions. She has an important role in expelling the foreign element from the family (Sarah) and gaining something from the father for the chosen male (Rebecca and Rachel). In the various portraits of the other feminine figures, Ruth is the most striking as faithful Israel that must recognize the foreignness, the otherness, of its own origins. The use of the key word "sûb" (turn, return) in ch. 1 of Ruth again recalls the imaginative structure of exile. The "return" of Naomi, who is herself a Judean, is accompanied by the "turning" of Ruth the Moabitess to Israel.

As for our contemporary historical contexts, it is not my argument here that these biblical images of the feminine can be simply . or mechanically appropriated by individuals or groups. The key is not for a given woman to see herself as Sarah or Judith or Ruth, but to try to meet the narrative thinking of the Bible in honest searching and questioning and to ask whether she can see herself in and through these narrative portraits. Or to revert to the figure of the mirror, Scripture must function as a "transparent" mirror, allowing one to see oneself but also to see through the image to what one is and may be. The same point applies for a male, or for any group that searches the Scripture. What is seen in and through the narrative portrayals may lead to the formation of a new image of the feminine - or to new images, for the interpretive seeds are many that can be planted.

There are so many obvious differences between biblical history and literature and our contemporary sensibilities and presuppositions in the western world, that a simple "transplanting" of meaning will not work. To take one example, our deeper assumptions about women and the feminine are bound to be changing because we have less need for a high birth rate, with a concomitant technology for both controlling and facilitating childbirth. This combination of technology and new social situation has simultaneously lessened the rigors of household management. These mutually reinforcing factors have made it emotionally and economically necessary for a great many women to pursue careers outside of home and marriage and to view themselves in terms of their employment. As more women enter the professions and the managerial side of business their economic and political power will increase. Now this shift is bound to induce a revised view of woman and the feminine, and there are no biblical models for this social-historical situation and the sense of historicity that is emerging. On the other hand, are there no inspiring and instructive images or pointers in the figure of Sarah seeking to fulfill her destiny as a woman? Or Hannah willing to put her greatest treasure, her son, in God's hands? Of Deborah who prophesies to Israel and leads in war? Of Judith who moves resolutely against Israel's foe through the use of her beauty and clever speech? Of Ruth who travels to a foreign country out of loyalty to an older woman, her mother-in-law? Even Mary, who seems so passive and submissive, is independent of human males as far as her vocation is concerned. In any case, the literary conventions employed in telling Mary's story in Matthew, Luke, and James signal to the reader that she should not be seen apart from a great cloud of witnesses, the other women who appear in this study.

However, since many experience this as a period of discontinuity with tradition when a simpler sort of recounting and extending of the biblical stories is particularly difficult, it may be that many serious biblical readers, whether lay or professional, should proceed aphoristically. As was pointed out in the first chapter, the narrative activity of storytelling requires making a "world" to be represented, and one must enter into that world, into that sequence of persons and events and that pattern of beliefs, in order to enjoy and understand it. The historical circumstances and historicity of biblical stories may be a "broken mirror" for many modern readers; that is, it may not be possible to enter into them and allow them to enter into one's own mind and heart to the point that they can reveal one's way in the world.

Of course, what I say raises the question whether my own exposition of biblical narrative thinking is possible. Doesn't this book itself, if it has any validity, affirm the possibility and value of interpreting and appropriating biblical stories? Yes and no. Yes, I have engaged in interpretation which I believe to be valid. But besides the fact that I am not a woman and cannot speak for any women, this book is not a task in which the meaning of my existence is at stake. Though I approach biblical literature as a critical believer and believing critic, the critical and theoretical nature of the project is different from the kind of existentially religious interpretation in which one finds or confirms one's way. If the book is a preparation or prolegomenon to better self-understanding and faith, or if it enriches anyone's life, well and good.

But self-understanding and faith may for many women be best served, not by a close attachment to the biblical stories per se, but by a mode of aphoristic reflection on biblical narrative. Aphorism as a genre of conflict or transition may cast up a provisional bridge to some new age or some new self. Between the narrative thinking of a new order in Sarah and a new realization of beauty and nurture one might identify oneself with aphoristic glimpses of the promise to Sarah.

And Sarah laughed ... and bore He-laughs ....
Everyone who hears will laugh for me ....

Or of Rebecca's courage, firmness, and daring.

I will go ....
Upon me your curse, my son, only
listen to my voice ....

Or of Deborah's charismatic authority.

ᶜûrî ᶜûrî dᵉbôrâ
ᶜûrî ᶜûrî dabbrî sîr
Awake, O Deborah, sing a song!

Or of the incredible decision of Ruth:

How you left your father and mother
and the land of your birth ....

An aphoristic procedure may be the way from "God to God," from the God whom we thought we left behind on the road to the God who is present urging us on to find him around the next bend. The aphoristic stance tells you that you can know, understand, and say something about God and humankind - but not too much. After all,

A person's mind mind minds her way,
But Yahweh steers her step.   [Prov 16.9][7]

Emily Dickinson, that great aphoristic poetess, knew that even as she rejected the God of her old self and was impelled toward a new feminine, divine Self, the movement from the old God of the puritan world view to the new God of the poetic self could take place only in, with, and through that same divine reality.

Old the grace, but new the Subjects -
Old, indeed, the East,
Yet upon His Purple Programme
Every Dawn, is first.   [#839]

2. Israel As A Way of Being in the World

"Israel" is a name that cannot be disembodied; it signifies always a concrete people in the world whose tradition includes the land of the ancestors. Yet here is the crucial paradox: the concreteness of Israel as people does not belie the essential meaning of the name and the people, which is first, last, and always a way of being in the world. "Jacob

127

shall no longer be your name but Israel, for you have struggled with God and with men, and you have prevailed" (Gen 32.29). Israel is a new humanity on the boundary, about to pass over the ford or through the waters; a new being centered in covenant with the God that guides its wandering; a landless people that have not yet entered their land (conclusion of Torah) and have had to leave it (conclusion of Former Prophets).

The meaning of Israel as the covenant people of God is strikingly analogous to the functions of the feminine and language. If one struggles with both God and men, one must be in between the two, or an "outsider" to both. Israel is the in between reality of God and man, the other side of both, a kind of word, a sort of language, which God speaks to the world and the world speaks to God. In relation to God Israel is that human aspect of "world" that God approaches, that hears and speaks to the divine reality, that is the agent of blessing or curse for the families of the earth (Gen 12.3). Israel prevails in the arena between God and men, as Abraham in Gerar and Jacob at the Jabbok. Israel brings new life for its foreign setting even as God's providence leads through an ironic tissue of events to the survival of Israel (Joseph in Egypt). As happens to the wife as sister, foreign kings and powers seek to possess Israel. As in the betrothal scenes, Israel's beginnings must be established in foreign lands. As in the promises to the barren wife, Israel can conceive its continuation and meaning only through the divine creation of its life.

There are many biblical narratives in which Israel, often through her representative figures, is the intercessor and sometimes a source of blessing for others. Abraham intercedes on behalf of Sodom and Gomorrah (Gen 18.18-35) and his prayer restores fertility to the household of Abimelech (20.17-18). Abimelech and one of his officials affirm to Abraham and Isaac that God is with them (Gen 21.22; 26.28). Jacob avows and Laban evidently agrees that Laban has been prospered by Yahweh due to Jacob's presence (30.30), and Jacob brings a "blessing" to Esau (33.11).

There is no need to rehearse the benefits that Joseph's service produces for the Egyptians. If the story of Joseph focuses on what Israel gives to Egypt through Joseph, who enables the people Israel to survive in a new land, the exodus story stresses the separation of Israel from Egypt. Indeed, the Hebrews despoil the Egyptians (Ex 12.36), but even in this context the king commands Moses and Aaron, "Be gone and bless me, too" (12.33). Egypt's problem was that it <u>did not know</u> Israel: "And a new king arose over Egypt who did not know Joseph" (1.8). I have already commented on the theme of knowledge and recognition in the Joseph story. The brothers deceive their father into thinking that in recognizing Joseph's coat he knows of his death. While Joseph is enslaved in Egypt Judah continues to act blindly, not recognizing Tamar as his daughter-in-law and eventually being forced to recognize the tokens of how he has wronged her. When the brothers travel to Egypt the first time, Joseph recognizes them, but they don't know who he is. The dénouement occurs during the second visit when Judah emotionally recounts his father's grief over Joseph and the fatal blow that the loss of Benjamin would be, accepts the fact that his father favors Rachel's sons over the rest of them, and offers himself as a ransom for Benjamin. Then Joseph makes himself known to his brothers. When Egypt no longer knows Joseph, Yahweh reveals to Moses that he knows the sufferings of his people (Ex 3.7). The narrative thinking of the Torah thus acknowledges Israel's dependence on Egypt, yet when Egypt loses knowledge of Israel Egypt is despoiled.

As a people coming out of other peoples yet "holy" - set aside - as a people struggling to win its way in the world bearing both beauty and vulnerability, Israel is like the arche-mother. She is source of life, object of love and inspiration, and agent of change. And like the militant woman she may have to become belligerent, but it is the roles and knowledge associated with the feminine that save her: wifely hospitality, motherly guidance, beauty, clever speech. Like Ruth, however, her origins are rooted in that very foreign reality from which she has separated herself. She too is a foreigner from the east that has come to dwell under Yahweh's wings, she too knows her identiyy in terms of a daring journey and the ability to turn opportunities into blessings. She reveals and conceals; she is part of the larger, sometimes hostile world, but distinct from it; she dwells at the border of Canaan and the boundary of the covenant mountain whether she is actually in the land of Canaan or some foreign land. She is thus the sign of the One who has a name, but a name which is not a proper proper name; of the One who shows himself, but shows himself as unseeable; of the One who is a presence in absence and absence in presence. Israel vis-à-vis God and the peoples is the symbolic

129

analogue as a covenant people to the self-other opposition that grounds language and that language mediates. The primary non- linguistic expression of this opposition in human existence is sexuality. The feminine, like language as a mediating capacity, is particularly associated with the side of the self turned toward the other and of the other turned toward the self.

One more question. If Israel's way of being in the world is analogous to the boundary situation of word and woman in our texts, does this mean that the God of this word and woman is "male"? First of all, it may be held that to some extent the great women of Israel's story are analogous to aspects of the divine reality. Within the sphere of human expression in symbol and story Yahweh, like the arche-mother, is the source of Israel's being, the object of love and inspiration, and the one who brings about change. His designs and acts are often extremely ambiguous. For example, why the prohibition of eating the fruit of the tree of knowledge of good and evil in Gen 2? Why would Yahweh Elohim simply not prevent Adam from ever approaching it? The prohibition raises the question of enhancement of life (immortality?) and opens the way to disobedience. Does the serpent not lead the man and woman astray? Since he is one of God's creatures, what kind of world has been created? The story itself does not answer these questions. It expresses instead the ambiguities and necessities that are primordial and universal in human experience, while affirming human responsibility in relation to God and world. Why does God's providence, as interpreted by Joseph, have to lead through familial strife and a breach of the most elementary fraternal morality to the saving of Egypt and Israel? Why does Yahweh continually harden the heart of the pharaoh in the Exodus plague narratives? Is it not trickery whereby Yahweh executes the rabble who desire meat in the desert? (See Nu 11.4-6, 18-23, 31-34.) Why does Yahweh send a "lying spirit" to speak through the prophets of Ahab? (I Kings 22.22) Is it an outbreak of divine demonism when Yahweh seeks to kill Moses as the latter returns to Egypt on the very mission on which Yahweh had sent him? (Ex 4.24-26)

In the instances cited, and others, we have to reckon with the ambiguity of the divine reality from the human stand-point within language. Narrative itself requires a lack or conflict in order for it to become genuinely "story," and in biblical narratives the ever present or presupposed subject,

God, must be associated with this lack or conflict in some manner or he could not participate in the story. Moreover, given the world as it is, with human alienation, idolatry, and great capacities for creation and destruction within the conditions of mortality, both concealing and revealing, deception and honesty are necessary to the realization of Yahweh's intentions for his greatest treasure, the new order of humanity as represented in Israel. So, as in the stories of the arche-mother and other valorous women, concealment and deception are part of the narrative thinking of the God of Israel. If a deeper view of the narrative process is taken, I think it may be argued that the biblical God is just as much "feminine" as "masculine."

But the second and essential thing to say is that the God of Israel is <u>transcendent</u>. Neither male nor female, God is utterly other than Israel and humankind, yet the "presence" that is most what humanness is. As already acknowledged, masculine verbal images are more common in Scripture's language about God than feminine. The image of marriage, with Israel as the bride of Yahweh, becomes a significant metaphor in Hosea's interpretation of God and Israel. For the rabbis the male lover in the Song of Songs is a symbol of God in relation to Israel; in the christian tradition he is a symbol of the Christ as the husband of the church. Granting all this, we have still dealt only with the surface level of metaphors and texts. From a religious and theological standpoint, Israel as a way of being in the world must say something essential about God. This "essential" word is first that there is no word finally adequate to express God's reality, but nonetheless God and Israel go together. Knowledge of one is knowledge of the other. Glory, covenants, law, promises - all were given to Israel (Romans 3.2; 9.4). The vehicle chosen and the message given say something also about the giver of the message. To hold that the God of Israel is simply the male counterpart, albeit transcendent, of the female Israel is to miss the recurring witnesses and intimations that the God of Israel is also being on the boundary: the God of places and times in between, being revealed at borders, on mountains between heaven and earth, giving promises and visions to live in and toward. This God's name is a proper name that is not proper, it cannot ultimately belong to the person because the Person cannot be owned by it (Ex 3.13-15). The God of Israel is a "face" which speaks to Moses's face, but which Moses cannot see (Ex 33.11, 23). The God of Israel is the God of the in-between, he cannot be "placed" either in Egypt, Mesopotamia, or Canaan (Josh 24.14-15), being a wanderer in a tent (II Sam 7.6). As being on the boundary, the God of Israel is the reality that both links and transcends the masculine and the feminine.

In order to survive Israel became like the nations and Yahweh became like other gods in the David-Zion tradition. Land, kingship, temple, the everlasting dynasty of David - these are important in the dialectic whereby Israel had to become like other nations in order to survive and be different.[8] But the imaginative structure of the Hebrew Scriptures is a field of metaphoric tensions between the border of the promised land and exile in foreign territory, and it is in this field of play that the transcendent God is disclosed. If this God appears more often in masculine guise than feminine, this simply has to do with the conditioning of the verbal level of language by historical context. But the metaphor is cleverer than its author (Lichtenberg), the self in its totality is more than any social construction thereof (Berger), and above all, the God of Israel is more than any sexual appellation or images that may be used.

The fundamental theological question is not whether God is male or female, masculine or feminine, but how we ourselves, here and now, in all our genders and genres, may come to know ourselves in relation to the One who is other than what we are and yet the Source and End of what we are and what we may become.

NOTES
BIBLIOGRAPHY
INDEXES

NOTES

NOTES TO CHAPTER I

On Biblical Narrative

1   See the major part of the Beardslee bibliography on proverb and aphorism in Williams, 1981: 113-14. See also Priest for discussion and references.

2   Quoted in Neumann, 1976b: 290.

3   Cited in Hammerskjöld: 3.

4   Note the common etymology of "story" and "history"; cf. German "Geschichte," which means both.

5   Robertson's understanding of paradigm shifts and his statement about "frames of reference" published in 1982 indicate that he should be in partial agreement, at least, with what I say here. His concepts are rooted in awareness of historical relativity and are confirmed by historical study that is philosophically oriented. There may be a contradiction in Robertson's position. On historical-genetic and literary-structural approaches, cf. Polzin, 1980: 3-7 and Crossan, 1982: 203-209.

6   One could reverse the argument for historical criticism: literary analysis is its necessary condition in order to determine what sort of text one is dealing with. See Crossan in Polzin, 1982 on the operational priority of structural or synchronic analysis.

7   Most of my translations of biblical texts will be more or less literal in order to indicate the fast-paced paratactic style of biblical prose. One of the chief features of this style is the sequence of parallel clauses and sentences connected only by "and." See Alter: 26.

8   Webster's Third New International Dictionary: "from OE rǣdan, akin to OE raed advice, counsel, OHG rātan to advise ...." (1889).

9   I have in mind also what he says about narration, especially "omniscience and inobtrusiveness" (183-85 and throughout the book). However, my approach to narration is stated in parts A and B.3. of this chapter.

10   Werke, vol. 2, Schriften zur Bibel (Munich, 1964): 1131. Cited in Alter: 93 (his trans.).

11   In Gen 20 Sarah is quoted (v. 5). But this scarcely changes the picture of Sarah's passivity.

12   On "implied author" see Booth: 74-76. It refers not to the actual author, who cannot be totally deduced from his or her work. The author creates a sort of "second self" in the literary work and the reader builds up an image of the author through engagement with this second self as it is suggested by theme, style, tone, and technique.

13   Following Alter I formerly called this the "type-scene." Alter derived the term from W. Arend, Die typischen Szenen bei Homer (Berlin: Weidmannsche, 1933). Although the noun "type" qua adjective is all right, I prefer the small change to the adjective "typic" in keeping with Arend's "typisch." It is an adjective, it avoids the current connotation of "typical" that might suggest the scene is typical of some larger segment of

Scripture or Scripture as a whole, but it also points to set patterns of certain scenes. These patterns are significant in my thesis concerning narrative thinking.

NOTES TO CHAPTER II

The Arche-Mother

1   So what von Rad has said of the proverbs of the wise holds true, mutatis mutandis, for aspects of narrative thinking: " ... For the men of old it was precisely the breakthrough to the generally and universally valid that was the most important thing." (1962: 420).

2   The association of Moses with water is too frequent to be accidental. Besides the two instances mentioned, there are also the first two plagues (Ex 7.8-8.11), the crossing of the Sea of Reeds (Ex 14), the waters of Meribah and Elim (15.22-27), and the incident of the water from the rock in Kadesh (Nu 20.1-13).

3   I say almost, because it is precisely one of the paradoxical aspects of the babylonian Isaiah's servant of Yahweh that he is disfigured (Isa 52.14; 53.2). Probably the prophet's vision of a new Israel involved the countering of this ancient code as he expressed new insight into the relation of God, Israel and the nations.

4   The wife-sister theme in Gen 20 probably also intimates in a kind of symbolic code that Abraham and Sarah are, from the israelite point of view, a "royal" couple. As mates and siblings they are like gods, heroes, and royal families. See Williams, 1980a: 112.

5   It is possible that Sarah's great beauty is not mentioned in Gen 20 because she is supposed to be old. There is not, of course, great consistency on this point, for why would the king of Gerar have taken her into his harem had she not been young and beautiful?

6   Since "kā^{c}ēt hayyâ," "at the reviving time," occurs also in Gen 18.10 historico-genetic criticism would, according to its own logic, ask whether one passage is dependent on the other. But this may have been a stock phrase appropriate for use in the typic scene convention.

7   There are, of course, many exceptions. See Brueggemann: 761-64. Also my exposition of Ruth ch. 3 and the concluding comment on Israel as a way of being in the world (ch. V, C.2.).

8   After the typic scene in Gen 26 Abimelech and company tell Isaac, "We have clearly seen that Yahweh was with you ...." (v. 28) See Polzin, 1975, for a structural view of the transformations in Gen 12, 20, and 26.

9   Older and younger are placed within quotation marks because there is an ambiguity in the message of the oracle. See Williams, 1978: 252-53.

10   Jacob's physical characteristic of smooth skin is probably meant to suggest that he is a "smoothie" in contrast to the hairy Esau, especially since the phrase is "ʔîš ḥālāq," "smooth man." (v. 11). Esau is a hunter who lives "outside," whereas Jacob is a shepherd semi-nomad who lives in a tent. Some of the thematic oppositions are suggested by plays on sounds. E.g., the favored "ṣā^{c}îr" (younger, smaller) displaces the "śā^{c}îr" (hairy one) who becomes "ś^e^{c}îr" (Seir or Edom).

11   Unless the story simply intends to indicate how there came to be "strange gods" with the family of Jacob (Gen 35.2), they should be construed as objects of veneration and transmitters of power. Laban calls them "my gods" (v. 30).

12   See Hugh White's essay, which is a form critical and tradition historical analysis.

13   I mean by "order" an orienting form that conveys and evokes a sense of being centered, a sense of harmony, although this harmony is a balance of dynamic tensions. I once heard Charles Harshorne define value as the harmony and intensity of experience. Without intensity - contrast and tension - there would be no satisfaction and no gain, no relief, or (aesthetically considered) no pleasure. But without harmony there would be not only lack of gain and satisfaction, but eventually chaos and dissolution. Thus my understanding of order includes a dynamic element, although I place a necessary emphasis upon orientation and harmony.

14   Or "of the steppeland." See S. Gevirtz: 43.

NOTES TO CHAPTER III

Other Feminine Figures

1   Donaldson has shown that the relationship of the patriarchs and their women move from incest (too close - Abraham and Sarah) and exogamy (too far - Abraham and Hagar) through parallel cousins (related through parent of same sex - Isaac-Rebecca) to cross-cousins (related through parent of opposite sex - Jacob-Rachel and Leah). The latter is just right according to C. Lévi-Strauss's analysis in Elementary Structures of Kinship. Two comments on the relevance of Donaldson's thesis to this book. (1) The conflict between exogamy (Hagar) and incest (Sarah) harmonizes nicely with my argument. The danger of "too close" is, however, necessary if Israel is to be able to view itself in the tradition as "one," as one flesh or of common ancestry. (2) It is interesting that the stories move back to exogamy after Jacob, in that Judah takes a canaanite wife (Gen 38.1) and Joseph marries the daughter of an egyptian priest (Gen 42.45), by whom he sires Manasseh and Ephraïm.

2   Even though Jacob's marriages with Leah and Rachel are just right according to Donaldson's structural analysis and the marriage of cousins is permitted in levitical law, he nevertheless transgresses the interdiction of union with a wife's sister while the first wife is still alive (Lev 18.18).

3   Besides Ju 4-5 there are also Delilah and Jephthah's daughter. Samson's mother in Ju 13 has been treated as one of the arche-mothers, although perhaps this classification should be qualified. The arche-mother gives birth to a special ancestor or deliverer, but this divine intention for Samson is aborted by his volatile, headstrong tendencies. Samson's characteristics are a microcosm of Israel according to Judges.

4   Any moral question about Jael's deed is germane only if it is interpreted outside of the world that the story circumscribes. It is not a tale recommending a morality for ordinary circumstances or even for the context of war. It tells rather how the powerful canaanite commander was undone by his own assumptions: that he could successfully fight against Israel contrary to Yahweh's will and that he could count on a woman to do his bidding.

5   The tale of Jephthah and his daughter is also relevant to this intention of the narrative. Although no disapproval is expressed concerning Jephthah's vow, the narrative relates that even the successful leader may be humbled. As Jephthah cries out when his daughter is the first person to meet him,

"Alas, my daughter! How you have brought me down low, and you - you are my source of sorrow! For I myself opened my mouth to Yahweh, and I cannot go back." [11.35]

6   Whether or not Haman is derived from "hāman," which is a hapaxlegomenon (Ezek 5.7), the narrator certainly plays on the similarity of sound between the proper name and "hēmâ," "wrath" (3.5; 7.10).

7   I am using the text as collated and translated by B. L. Daniels in Dungan and Cartlidge: 11-26.

8   The woman in Ju 14 falls outside of my frame of reference because she does not have directly to do with Israel's destiny, and she does not "seduce" (lead astray) the man in the same fashion that Delilah does and the wife of Potiphar seeks to do. The story does, however, tell us that Samson is subject to enticement, a foreshadowing of his surrender to Delilah's enticement (note "pattî" in 14.15 and 16.5). See Polzin's interpretation of the irony in ch. 14 (1980: 185-86).

NOTES TO CHAPTER IV

The Symbolic Functions of the Feminine

1   E.g., Gaster, Graves and Patai. Also Hooke, who understands myth primarily in terms of functions (ritual magic, etiology, recitation, etc.).

2   See Williams, 1981: 100-101 (n. 24) for my understanding of symbol. Also Perrin, esp. 29-30, who uses Wheelwright's distinction between "steno-symbol" and "tensive symbol." "Symbol" is deeper and more encompassing than "concept" and "theme," though the latter are included therein.

3   So are Paghat and the harlot in Gilgamesh, but they do not have the second and third features.

4   Moses has two "mothers" - his birth mother and the egyptian adoptive mother. Both are anonymous and neither is identified with his life after early infancy. That Moses has two mothers, yet lacks strong identification with either of them, is a narrative fact that forms part of the mystery of Moses. His birth and his death (Deut 34.6-7) are both out of the ordinary and shrouded in divine mystery.

5   And see further now on the thematic relationship between this episode and its larger context, Ackerman, 1982: esp. 103-107 (which appeared as this book went to press).

6   The author has David in mind if the genealogies in Ruth 4.18-22 and I Chron 2.5-15 are old, going back to the time of the composition of Gen 38.

NOTES TO CHAPTER V

The Biblical Feminine and
Contemporary Religious thought

1   By "opposition" I do not mean "contradiction." An opposition may become a contradiction if a split of opposing realities occurs. However, opposition means in this case a dialectical interplay between realities that are in tension or conflict, but that are also necessary to each other.

2   See M. Douglas on strong group, strong grid and strong group, weak grid.

3   I would include the nativity stories of Matthew and Luke in the jewish tradition, certainly from the point of view of literary genre and religious dynamics. See ch. 2, A.

4   In the primordial history the favored Abel is murdered by Cain.

5   Whatever the actual author's intention, the narrator would probably not have had an audience without this minimal recognition of accepted conventions.

6   As Schubert Ogden has said, "Rightly understood, the problem of God is not one problem among several others; it is the only problem there is" (1).

7   For my purposes in this context I have used "person" as a generic noun to render "ʔādām" in the hebrew text. My model is the usage of "personne" in french and "Person" in german. In both languages the noun is feminine, so that all words must show gender agreement (articles, modifying adjectives, pronouns) are likewise feminine when used with the word. "Une personne agée" (an old person); "eine männliche Person" (a male person).

8   As in the self-other relation one must participate in one's world in order to survive meaningfully and be different as an individual.

PERIODICAL ABBREVIATIONS

CBQ	Catholic Biblical Quarterly
HUCA	Hebrew Union College Annual
JAAR	Journal of the American Academy of Religion
Suppl.	Supplementary Issue
JBL	Journal of Biblical Literature
JJS	Journal of Jewish Studies
JSOT	Journal for the Study of the Old Testament
JQ	Jewish Quarterly
ZAW	Zeitschrift für die Alttestamentliche Wissenschaft

BIBLIOGRAPHY
(Works cited)

Ackerman, James S.
1982   "Joseph, Judah, and Jacob," in K. R. R. Gros Louis with J. S.
        Ackerman, eds., Literary Interpretations of Biblical Narratives.
        Volume II: 85-113. Abingdon: Nashville.
Allemann, B.
1967   "Metaphor and Antimetaphor," in S. R. Hopper and D. L. Miller,
        eds., Interpretation: the Poetry of Meaning: 103-23. NY: Har-
        court, Brace and World.
Alter, Robert
1981   The Art of Biblical Narrative. NY: Basic Books.
Arend, Walther
1933   Die typischen Szenen bei Homer. Forschungen zur klassischen
        Philologie 7. Berlin: Weidmannsche.
Aristotle
        Aristotle's Poetics, tr. S. H. Butcher, intro. F. Fergusson. NY:
        Hill and Wang, 1961.
Beardslee, William
1970   Literary Criticism of the New Testament. Phila.: Fortress.
Berger, Peter
1969   The Sacred Canopy: Elements of A Sociologocial Theory of Re-
        ligion. Garden City, NY: Doubleday.
Boman, T.
1960   Hebrew Thought Compared with Greek, tr. J. L. Moreau. Phila.:
        Westminster.
Booth, Wayne C.
1961   The Rhetoric of Fiction. Chicago: Univ. Press.
Bradstreet, Anne
1967   The Works of Anne Bradstreet, ed. J. Hensley. Cambridge,
        Mass.: Belknap for Harvard U. Press (Second ed. of Bradstreet's
        poems printed posthumously in 1678).
Bright, John
1965   Jeremiah, Anchor Bible 21. Garden City, NY: Doubleday.
Brueggemann, Walter
1977   "Israel's Social Criticism and Yahweh's Sexuality," JAAR 45
        Suppl. (1977): 739-72.
Carlston, C. E.
1980   "Proverbs, Maxims, and the Historical Jesus," JBL: 87-105.
Clines, D. J. A.
1981   "Nehemiah 10 as an Example of Early Jewish Biblical Exegesis,"
        JSOT 21: 111-17.
Coats, George W.
1976   From Canaan to Egypt: Structural and Theological Context for
        the Joseph Story. CBQ Monograph Series 4. Washington: Cath-
        olic Biblical Association.
Colwell, E. C.
1970   New or Old: The Christian Struggle with Change and Tradition.
        Phila.: Westminster.

Coogan, Morton D.
1978   ed. and tr., Stories from Ancient Canaan. Phila.: Westminster.
Craven, Toni
1977   "Artistry and Faith in the Book of Judith," Semeia 8: 75-101.
Crenshaw, James L.
1978   Samson: A Secret Betrayed, A Vow Ignored. Atlanta: John Knox.
Crossan, John Dominic
1973   In Parables: The Challenge of the Historical Jesus. NY: Harper and Row.
1976   Raid on the Articulate: Comic Eschatology in Jesus and Borges. NY: Harper and Row.
1982   "'Ruth Amid the Alien Corn': Perspectives and Methods in Contemporary Biblical Criticism," in Polzin, 1982 (see Polzin): 199-210.
Culley, Robert C.
1976   Studies in the Structure of Biblical Narrative. Phila.: Fortress.
Dickinson, Emily
1968   The Complete Poems of Emily Dickinson, ed. T. H. Johnson (Boston, Ontario: Little, Brown).
Donaldson, M. E.
1981   "Kinship Theory in the Patriarchal Narratives: The Case of the Barren Wife," JAAR 49: 77-87.
Douglas, Ann
1977   The Feminization of American Culture. NY: Avon.
Douglas, Mary
1973   Natural Symbols. NY: Pelican and Random.
Dungan, D. L. and Cartlidge, D. R.
1974   Sourcebook of Texts for the Comparative Study of the Gospels, 4th ed. Missoula, Montana: Scholars.
Dunne, John
1965   The City of the Gods: A Study in Myth and Mortality. NY: Macmillan.
Fishbane, Michael
1975   "Composition and Structure in the Jacob Cycle," JJS 26: 15-38.
Fitzgerald, F. Scott
1953   The Great Gatsby. NY: Scribner's (orig. cop. 1925).
Fohrer, Georg
1963   Das Buch Hiob, KAT 16. Gütersloh: Mohn.
Fokkelman, J. P.
1975   Narrative Art in Genesis. Assen/Amsterdam: van Gorcum.
Frankfort, H., et al
1946   The Intellectual Adventure of Ancient Man. Chicago: Univ. Press.
Gaster, Th.
1961   Thespis. 2nd rev. ed. Garden City, NY: Doubleday.
Gevirtz, Stanley
1975   "Of Patriarchs and Puns: Joseph at the Fountain, Jacob at the Ford," HUCA 46: 33-54.
Graves, R. and Patai, R.
1963   Hebrew Myths: The Book of Genesis. NY: McGraw-Hill.
Greeley, A. M.
1977   The Mary Myth: On the Femininity of God. NY: Seabury.
Hammerskjöld, Dag
1965   Markings. NY: Knopf.

Hawthorne, Nathaniel
1967   The Scarlet Letter in Great Short Works of Nathaniel Haw-
           thorne. NY: Harper and Row.

Hooke, S. H.
1976   Middle Eastern Mythology. NY: Penguin.

Kafka, Franz
1953   "Betrachtungen," in Hochzeitsvorbereitungen auf dem Lande
           und andere Prosa aus dem Nachlass, ed. M. Brod. NY: Schocken.

Kerényi, Carl
1963   "Prolegomena," in C. G. Jung and Kerényi, Essays on a Science
           of Mythology, tr. R. F. C. Hull: 1-24. NY: Harper TB.

Landy, Francis
1980   "Humour in the Bible," JQ 27: 13-19.

Kermode, Frank
1977   The Sense of An Ending: Studies in the Theory of Fiction. NY:
           Oxford.

Lec, Stanislaw J.
1964   Unfrisierte Gedanken, ed. K. Dedecius. München: Hanser.

Lichtenberg, G. C.
1968,   1971. Schriften und Briefe: Sudelbücher, ed. W. Promies. (Mün-
           chen: Hanser).

MacDonald, Duncan B.
1936   The Hebrew Philosophical Genius. Princeton: Univ. Press.

Miller, David L.
1970   Gods and Games: Toward a Theology of Play. NY and Cleveland:
           World.

Neumann, Gerhard
1973   "Umkehrung und Ablenkung: Franz Kafkas 'gleitendes Paradox,'"
           in H. Politzer, ed., Franz Kafka, Wege der Forschung, Bd. 322.
           Darmstadt: Wissenschaftliche Buchgesellschaft.

1976a   ed., Der Aphorismus: Zur Geschichte, zu den Formen und Mög-
           lichkeiten einer literarischen Gattung. Darmstadt: Wissen-
           schaftliche.

1976b   Ideenparadiese: Untersuchungen zur Aphoristik von Lichtenberg,
           Novalis, Fr. Schlegel und Goethe. München: Fink.

Nohrnberg, James
1981   "Moses," in B. O. Long, ed., Images of Man and God: Old Test-
           ament Short Stories in Literary Focus: 35-57. Sheffield: Almond.

Ogden, Schubert M.
1966   The Reality of God and Other Essays. NY: Harper and Row.

Perrin, Norman
1976   Jesus and the Language of the Kingdom. Phila.: Fortress.

Polzin, Robert
1975   "The 'Ancestress of Israel in Danger' in Danger," Semeia 3:
           81-98.

1980   Moses and the Deuteronomist: A Literary Study of the Deut-
           eronomic History. NY: Seabury.

1982   ed. with E. Rothman, The Biblical Mosaic: Changing Perspec-
           tives (Semeia Studies) Philadelphia: Fortress.

Pope, Marvin
1965   Job, Anchor Bible 15. Garden City, NY: Doubleday.

Porterfield, Amanda
1980   Feminine Spirituality in America: From Sarah Edwards to
           Martha Graham. Phila.: Temple Univ.

Priest, J. F.
1968   "Humanism, Skepticism, and Pessimism in Israel," JAAR 36:
        311-26.
Pritchard, James
1955   ed., Ancient Near Eastern Texts Pertaining to the Old Tes-
        tament, 2nd ed. Princeton: Univ. Press.
Rad, Gerhard von
1962,   1965. Old Testament Theology, I and II, tr. D. M. G. Stalker.
        NY: Harper and Row.
1972a   Genesis: A Commentary, rev. ed. Phila.: Westminster.
1972b   Wisdom in Israel. Nashville: Abingdon.
Ricoeur, Paul
1978   "The Narrative Function," Semeia 13: 177-202.
Robertson, David
1977   The Old Testament and the Literary Critic. Phila.: Fortress.
1982   "Micaiah ben Imlah: A Literary View," in Polzin, 1982 (See
        Polzin): 139-46.
Rogerson, J. W.
1974   Myth in Old Testament Interpretation. Berlin: de Gruyter.
Sanders, James A.
1972   Torah and Canon. Phila.: Fortress.
Schneidau, Herbert N.
1977   Sacred Discontent: The Bible and Western Tradition. Baton
        Rouge, La.: Louisiana State Univ. Press.
Speiser, E. A.
1964   Genesis, Anchor Bible 1. Garden City, NY: Doubleday.
Tillich, Paul
1951   Systematic Theology, vol. 1. Chicago: Univ. Press.
Trible, Phyllis
1978   God and the Rhetoric of Sexuality. Phila.: Fortress.
Vawter, Bruce
1980   "Proverbs 8:22: Wisdom and Creation," JBL 99: 205-16.
Watts, Alan W.
1968   Myth and Ritual in Christianity. Boston: Beacon.
Webster's
1961   Webster's Third New International Dictionary. Springfield,
        Mass.: Merriam and Co.
White, Hugh
1979   "The Initiation Legend of Isaac," ZAW 91:1-30.
Williams, James G.
1978   "The Comedy of Jacob: A Literary Study," JAAR 46 Supp.:
        241-66.
1979   "Number Symbolism and Joseph As Symbol of Completion," JBL
        98: 86-87.
1980a   "The Beautiful and the Barren: Conventions in Biblical Type-
        Scenes," JSOT 17:107-19.
1980b   "The Power of Form: A Study of Biblical Proverbs," Semeia 17:
        35-58.
1981   Those Who Ponder Proverbs: Aphoristic Thinking and Biblical
        Literature. Sheffield: Almond.
Wolff, H. W.
1964   "Die Begründungen der prophetischen Heils- und Unheils-
        sprüche," in Gesammelte Studien zum Alten Testament: 9-35.
        München: Kaiser.

INDEX OF BIBLICAL REFERENCES

[* = principal discussions]

A Selective
INDEX OF BIBLICAL NAMES

[* = principal discussions]

INDEX OF AUTHORS